139813
£3.95

KT-463-289

Past-into-Present Series

THE FAMILY

Alan Dures

B.T.BATSFORD LTD

London

First published 1978
© Alan Dures 1978

ISBN 0 7134 3277 2

Printed in Great Britain by
Cox & Wyman Ltd, Fakenham
for the Publishers B.T. Batsford Ltd,
4 Fitzhardinge Street, London W1H 0AH

Acknowledgment

The Author and Publishers would like to thank the following for their kind permission to reproduce copyright illustrations: T & R Annan & Son Ltd for fig 56; Associated Press Ltd for fig 60; the BBC for fig 58; the British Library for fig 6; Camera Press for fig 61; the Central Office of Information for fig 59; Corpus Christi College, Cambridge, for fig 7; the Greater London Council for fig 47; the Imperial War Museum for figs 42 and 53; the Mansell Collection for figs 1, 8-12, 14-16, 20, 22, 26, 27, 29, 33, 34 and 46; the National Portrait Gallery for fig 28; the Radio Times Hulton Picture Library for figs 3, 17, 18, 21, 25, 30, 36, 37, 39, 40, 41, 43-5, 50-2, 54-5 and 57; the Royal Academy of Arts for fig 48; the Tate Gallery for fig 35; and the Wellcome Trustees for fig 38. The other illustrations appearing in the book are the property of the Publishers.

Contents

The Illustrations

Introduction

The family is the only social institution, other than religion, which is formally developed in all societies. Almost everyone is born into a family, and most people found a family of their own. It is difficult to escape from the ties and obligations of family, whereas religious or political duties are laid aside by many people. Almost no family role can be delegated to others, as can happen to duties at work.

Throughout history many writers and thinkers have given prominence to the family. Confucius, the Chinese philosopher born c. 551 B.C., thought that happiness and prosperity would prevail in a society if only everyone would behave 'correctly' as a family member, which meant primarily that no one should fail in his family obligations. Similarly, much of the early Hebrew writing in Exodus, Deuteronomy, Ecclesiastes, the Psalms and Proverbs is also devoted to the importance of obeying family rules. In India, too, the earliest literature, the *Rig-Veda,* codified about the latter half of the second millennium B.C., gives a great deal of attention to the family.

What is also significant is that revolutions, real or imagined, have generally tried to modify or abolish the family. Plato, the Greek philosopher (c. 428-348 B.C.), outlined an imaginary new society in his work the *Republic,* in which the family was abolished because it gave unfair advantage to some over others. For Plato's top members of society — his 'Guardians' — family conditions were entirely regulated. Conception would take place at the same time each year at certain 'festivals'. Children born out of season would be eliminated, as would those born defective. All children would be taken from their parents at birth and reared under vigorous conditions to 'fit' them for high office.

Of course Plato's Republic never existed, but modern organizations such as the Israeli *kibbutz* and the Russian *kolkhoz* have tried to modify the family and give more stress to communal living. Under these arrangements mothers do a full working day, and though children see their parents at regular intervals they are encouraged to look to their nursery attendant as 'mother' during working hours. But the evidence available suggests that since their beginning there has been a move towards a more usual family arrangement, particularly as regards mothers' insistence upon seeing more of their children.

1   The residence of a Saxon nobleman, showing a considerable number of servants and also a number of fighting men belonging to the lord.

2   In a noble household cooking had to be done on a grand scale. Here we see a huge cooking pot and several beasts being roasted over a pit. The basting spoon is particularly large and bellows are used to keep the fire going.

1
The Medieval Family

The Anglo-Saxon Family

In the fifth century A.D. the Anglo-Saxons settled in England. What we know of existing laws and customs in Anglo-Saxon society suggests that the family was of the greatest importance. The community depended upon the family for the maintenance of peace and the punishment of crime. But in Anglo-Saxon times the family meant two different things. First the family was the larger group including all relatives and 'kin', which was called in Anglo-Saxon the 'maegth'. The smaller group, like our own nuclear family, consisted only of the husband, his wife and children. These two groups were really distinct, and the larger group, the kindred group, was in many ways the more important.

The importance of the kindred group can be seen from the fact that when a woman married she was not regarded as kin to her husband's maegth but remained in her own. If she committed a crime, her husband was not responsible for her — it was her father's kin who had to make compensation.

Members of the maegth were crucial to a man throughout his life. They were his witnesses and sureties at marriage. If he was taken to court, his kindred came to support him; if he lost the case, they would pay his fines. In a feud they stood beside him to defend him even with their lives. Even after death the importance of the kindred family continued. If a man had been murdered, his kin avenged his murder or exacted compensation for it. They acted as guardians of his widow and children and took charge of the estate until his children came of age. All of common blood were bound by these ties of mutual right and obligation.

If we turn to the smaller family group we find that in many many ways the rights of women in the family were greater under Anglo-Saxon law than in subsequent times up to the twentieth century. The property which a wife brought to the marriage never legally passed to her husband. If the wife died, her property reverted to the children, and only in the absence of children did it go to her husband. Conversely, if the husband died, all the property a wife had brought to the marriage came back to her, not to the sons, in addition to her 'morning gift', a piece of land specially set aside for her by her husband, or — in the absence of this — half her husband's property. If, however, the wife

3 Anglo-Saxon women of the eighth century. Anglo-Saxon women appear to have been freer, for example to ride unaccompanied, than women in the later medieval period.

did not remain 'faithful' for a year after her husband's death, she forfeited the morning gift, but after a year had elapsed she could take the gift to another marriage. Divorce appears to have been easier than in subsequent centuries. Moreover, the wife received half her husband's property if she took the children with her or a child's portion if these remained with her husband. If the wife was guilty of infidelity, however, the husband could divorce her and she suffered the loss of all property.

Children, too, seem to have enjoyed greater legal rights than in later times. Sons became legally independent at the age of about 15 after which they, and not their fathers, would inherit their mother's property should she die. It seems likely that a son would continue to live with his father until marriage, and the father administered his son's property. Also the father could require obedience of his son, as this was necessary for the well being of the household. But the son could leave the household and, for example, become a monk without the father's consent. Daughters had less freedom but, even so, once they came of age they had certain rights. They could enter a convent if they chose, or conversely they could no longer be forced to enter a convent or be given in marriage against their will. In later Anglo-Saxon law it would seem that even girls under the age of majority could not be married against their will.

The Norman Conquest: English Feudalism

A significant change in property laws and family relationships came with the development of a feudal structure after the Norman Conquest of 1066. Under a feudal structure each tenant or vassal held land of a feudal overlord, the king being the supreme overlord. Vassals owed strict obligations to their overlords such as providing a certain number of knights to fight for the lord. Each vassal had to take an oath of fealty to his lord when entering his property. The relationship between a vassal and his feudal overlord in many ways superseded that of 'blood' and 'kinship' ties, and became the most important relationship in medieval society, at least at the upper levels. The law placed restrictions on the division of family property. A father could grant 'portions' to his daughters for marriage, and some land to his younger sons, but the vast amount had to go to the eldest son, so that he had sufficient land and wealth to perform his duties — such as providing knights — to his feudal overlord. Thus the system known as primogeniture, in which the bulk of the father's wealth was inherited by the eldest son, became a feature of the English landed classes. This had profound effects on the family and society throughout English history.

The development of the English common law, under the influence of feudal customs, weakened family ties and diminished the importance of the family compared with the Anglo-Saxon period. Unlike some French laws, English common law did not recognize any of the political or military obligations of blood relationships; obligations to the feudal overlord were greater than to your blood relations in the family. In fact the common law gave the king and other lords a large amount of control over the family of their vassals. No woman, be she maid or widow, could marry without the consent of the lord. In the case of a maid, the consent of the father's lord was usually required, while a widow needed the agreement of her late husband's lord. Thus the lord could prevent the formation of family connections by his vassals which he thought undesirable or dangerous. Moreover if a vassal died and left a son under 21 or an unmarried daughter, the lord could marry them to whomsoever he pleased.

But, despite legal restrictions, families could still exercise a great deal of power, especially when they enjoyed real favour. The Clare family is a good example of family power and influence exercised over 200 years or more. Richard Fitz Gilbert de Clare came to England with William the Conqueror and married Rohese, sister of another great Norman baron, Walter Gifford. Richard was given a large fief (a feudal estate) in East Anglia and neighbouring counties. His sons were favourites of King Henry I and were subsequently given large forfeited baronies. Walter became the lord of extensive estates in the west of England while Robert received land in East Anglia and Essex. The family continued to prosper and grow in political power. By the early thirteenth century the Clares were a formidable political force. In 1215 the Clares played a significant role in the rebellion against King John; of the 24 barons chosen to enforce Magna Carta, no less than 16 were relatives of Richard, Earl of Clare, 13 of Clare blood and three relatives by marriage.

Non-Aristocratic Families

In medieval society a great number of families were in theory totally unfree. The villein or serf held his land in the village at the will of the lord. In practice, however, the villein was secure in his land if he paid his customary rents. When the villein died a member of his family inherited the land but, unlike the greatest landowners — the king's tenants-in-chief, the land did not always go to the eldest son. In the medieval village there were two main customs of inheritance. By *impartible inheritance* the land of the villager went to one son, either to the eldest son or, by a custom known as the 'borough English rule', to the younger son. In any case, one of his sons and only one of his sons inherited.

When a villager did not have any children, his land would pass to a relative, though not necessarily to his closest one. By a custom known as the 'blood of the village' the lord sometimes decided that a property should pass to a

4 *right*   Medieval babies were generally depicted as small adults, so these twins could be new born. The chances of the mother dying in childbirth were very high during this period.

5 *far right*   A scene of family tragedy as a husband and father dies.

blood relation. A thirteenth-century court, discussing the land of Thomas Arnold, decided that 'a certain Ralph Arnold, his brother, is the nearer heir by blood but they say that by the custom of the manor Nicholas, son of John, is nearer heir of the said Thomas in that John was of the blood of the Village'. Such a custom shows that the ties of kindred had declined since Anglo-Saxon times.

But in some counties, for example in Kent in around the thirteenth century, *partible inheritance* was the most common concept amongst villagers. This could mean that a man divided his land equally between his sons, or if he had no sons, daughters, or it could mean that the land was held in common among the family members. There were examples in the thirteenth century of land being held undivided for over 80 years. In such cases, brothers and their children would form an 'extended family', living in one large house or in a small group of adjoining houses. This family structure was also found outside Kent in parts of East Anglia and Wales. It seems to be found little after the thirteenth century though in certain parts of France it continued until the nineteenth century.

Size of Households

It would appear from the evidence of thirteenth-century documents that the average household in the village was small, occupied only (in the main) by one generation. For example, in a Lincolnshire village in the thirteenth century there was only one household where an uncle and aunt were part of the household. The households of the great baronial families, however, were different, though the size of such a household is a matter of some dispute. If all the retainers are counted, then such a household could run to over a hundred.

Moreover the household would include a number of children who had been sent there to be educated, though of course this was partly compensated for by the absence of the elder children in the family, who would have been sent away from home. The great baronial households would have a number of officials who saw to the smooth running of the household and estate. From the twelfth century such households became more permanent as the barons, like the kings, took up fixed abodes and stopped moving from one of their estates to another. But we should not be misled into seeing the medieval household as an extended family. There is little evidence to suggest that the household included a wide range of relatives: it was rather the servants — in the widest sense — of the lord, who contributed the bulk of the household. In that respect the medieval household was a unit of power and administration rather than a family organization.

The Paston Family

The Paston family was of relatively humble origins and in the fourteenth century Clement Paston was described as 'a good plain husbandman'. By the fifteenth century the Pastons owned large estates in East Anglia and were comfortable landed gentry. John Paston was head of the family in the mid-fifteenth century and he married Margaret Mautby; the marriage was a carefully-planned step in the further enriching of the Paston family, for Margaret brought with her the important manor of Mautby.

An examination of the family life of the Pastons tells us a good deal about relationships within the medieval family. The first point that strikes us is that Margaret had a chance to get to know her husband only after the marriage. It is hardly surprising, therefore, that the relationship between husband and wife seems to have been fairly formal. For example, Margaret's letters to her husband often began: 'Right reverend and worshipful sir, in my most humble voice I recommend me to you'; and frequently ended: 'your servant and bede-woman'. But we should not read too much into this conventional language, and Margaret's letters also show considerable affection towards her husband. She writes to him in London: 'Sir I pray you, if you tarry long at London, that it will please [you] to send for me, for I think [it] long since I lay in your arms'. John Paston was obviously a formal man, but he talks of his wife as 'my own dear sovereign lady', and writes with concern that 'John Hobbs tells me that you are sickly which melikes not to hear. Praying you heartily that you take what may do you ease and spare not'.

All comments about the relationship between husband and wife in the medieval period stress the wife's total subordination. Chaucer's Good Wife taught her daughter that a wife's attitude to her husband was to 'love thou him and honoure moost of erthelie thing'. Much medieval literature suggests that wives were frequently beaten and used in degrading ways, though in many a will a husband calls his wife 'my most trusty frende'.

6   Death was a much more constant threat to family life in the past than today. The Black Death of the mid-14th century carried off about a third of the European population and thereafter preoccupation with death was a theme of medieval paintings and writings. Here we see a depiction of Death (the skeleton-like figures in the central panel) pursuing its victims, and then the inevitable funeral.

Although the medieval wife was so subordinate to her husband, her role in the family often gave her considerable status. Most women of Margaret Paston's social rank conducted family business in their husbands' absence. Margaret Paston frequently represented her husband in law suits and in drawing up new agreements with tenants. In 1465 it was Margaret who defended the Manor of Drayton against the attack of the Duke of Suffolk. By the autumn of that year poor Margaret wrote to her husband of the 'sickness and trouble that I have had, I am brought right low and weak, but to my power I will do as well as I can or may in your matters'. The power which medieval women could acquire in family business is illustrated by Lady Isabel Berkeley. While

7 From a manuscript at Corpus Christi, Cambridge, showing a woman with her betrothed, while the discarded suitor refuses to give up.

8 Pilgrimage to Canterbury, based on Chaucer's *Canterbury Tales*. Pilgrimages and religious activities in general were one of the few respectable ways for women to escape from home in this period.

she was in London doing business for her husband she wrote home telling her husband to do nothing on the estate until she returned: 'keep well all about you till I come home, and treat not without me, and then all things shall be well'.

For the rich as well as the poor, a wife was essentially a housewife; her real function was the ordering and proper management of the home. This implied not only keeping the house clean and providing meals, but also arranging her supplies. In this she was far more dependent on her own efforts than the modern housewife. A lack of forethought on her part might well mean a lack of food for the family several months hence. It was necessary to buy in bulk and when the price was right, as Margaret Paston's bailiff stressed in a letter to her: 'Mistress, it were good to remember your stuff of herring now this fishing time. I have got me a friend in Lowestoft to help to buy me seven or eight barrels and [they] shall not cost me above 6s. 8d [33½p] a barrel . . . You shall do more now with 40 shillings' than you shall at Christmas with 5 marks [66s. 8d]'. Margaret Paston, like all good housewives, was conscious of prices. When her son was in London she tells him 'send me word what price a pound. If that be a better buy in London than it is here, I shall send you money to buy such stuff as I will have'.

Turning to the children in the family we can say that the relationship between parents and children was even more formal than that between husband and wife. Children had to give unquestioning obedience to their fathers, even when they were young adults, 'for daughters, grown women and sons, gentlemen of 30 and 40 years old, might not sit in their presence without leave but stood like mutes bare headed before them'. When the Paston children wrote to their father they opened with words such as: 'Most reverend and worshipful father I recommend me heartily and submit me lowly to your good fatherhood'. But in practice the children were not always so submissive. In 1459 John Paston offended his father with some act of independence, and four years later John was in trouble for leaving home without parental permission!

On both occasions the son had to give way, helped by his mother Margaret who begged her son to plead for forgiveness. 'Spare not to write to him (your father) again as lowly as you can beseeching him to be your good father'. Then Margaret wrote to her husband a simple plea for her son: 'For God's sake Sir, have pity on him'.

Though Margaret Paston interceded for her sons, her relations with her own daughters appear to have been none too good. She was constantly urging her eldest son, Sir John Paston, to find homes for her daughters in other families. Could he find some 'worshipful place' for the younger daughter Margery 'for we either of us weary of the other'. Again, on hearing that her eldest daughter might be returning home, Margaret asks Sir John if he can make other arrangements: 'for I shall be loth to send for her, and with me she shall only lose her time. Unless she will be better occupied she will often times move me, and put me in great unquietness'.

It was, in fact, common practice for children to be boarded out with other families. An Italian observer found this strange:

> The want of affection in the English is strongly manifested towards their children, for having kept them at home till they arrive at the age of seven or nine years at the utmost they put them out both males and females to hard service in the houses of other people, and few are born who are exempted from this fate, for everyone however rich he may be, sends away his children into the houses of others whilst he, in return, receives those of strangers into his own. And on enquiring the reason for the severity, they answered that they did it in order that their children might learn better manners.

Conclusion

Our evidence on family life in the Anglo-Saxon period is slight, but the laws concerning marriage and property suggest that the rights both of women and children were stronger in the Anglo-Saxon period than after the Norman Conquest. The increasing insistence on primogeniture under feudal law meant that wives and children were economically more dependent and consequently more submissive to the head of the family, either the father or the eldest son. By the later medieval period literary works such as Chaucer's *Canterbury Tales*, court cases such as *Early Chancery Proceedings* and above all correspondence such as the *Paston Letters*, enable us to gain an impression of family life. The picture that emerges is that relationships tended to be formal, even brutal; all members of the family were totally subordinate to the father. Discipline was harsh and obviously considered good for the forming of character. In the sixteenth century, at any rate, Lady Jane Grey considered her brutal upbringing a blessing. She wrote: 'one of the greatest benefits that God ever gave me is that he sent me so sharpe and severe Parentes'.

2
The Pre-Industrial Family
1500-1750

Aristocratic Families

In the sixteenth century the aristocratic family remained large, consisting not only of husband and wife but also of household officers — the gentlemen and gentlewomen in waiting, numerous guests and usually between 8 and 100 servants. In most cases the eldest son and his wife also spent the early years of their married life in the same house. But it is unlikely that any other relatives or grandparents would have been living there. Moreover the number of children in the family was not usually large. This was due to the high death rate both of children and mothers; a wife's chance of dying in the first 15 years of marriage was one in four, almost a quarter of the deaths being at childbirth. Of course many husbands married again. The first Duke of Newcastle's second wife knew exactly why the Duke had proposed to her:

> he having but two sons proposed to marry me, a young woman that might prove fruitful to him and increase his posterity by a masculine offspring.

There can be no doubt about the importance which the upper classes attributed to the family in this period. In the sixteenth century, especially among ancient families, obedience to head of the family and maintaining family honour was more important than obedience to the State. Thomas Earl of Arundel 'thought no other part of history so considerable as what related to his own family'. Pride in the family is reflected in the number of family histories, with their stress on heraldry (the family coat of arms) and genealogy (tracing the origins of the family). The Popham family in the sixteenth century claimed to be able to trace its origins back to Noah! William Cecil, Lord Burghley, traced his family back to the Welsh borders before the Norman Conquest, but his more hardheaded son Robert recognized that such claims were total nonsense.

How the Aristocracy Lived

During this period the houses of the aristocracy became more elaborate and comfortable. The greater desire for privacy was reflected in the building of bedrooms and private rooms as the communal great hall of the medieval castle declined. There was a spate of new country houses at the end of the sixteenth century. Robert Cecil, Earl of Salisbury, spent some £40,000 on Hatfield House between 1608 and 1612, and a contemporary wrote that 'no kingdom in the world spent so much in building as we did in King James's time'. The gentry and aristocratic family also drank and ate sumptuously. In

9 Robert Cecil, Earl of Salisbury. He realised the importance of a good marriage and family connections. His father, William Cecil, had built up the family fortunes and ensured that his son Robert became the most important minister in England. Robert endeavoured to pass on good advice about marriage to his sons.

10 Hatfield House (as it was at the end of the 17th century). By the 16th and 17th centuries the upper classes were building homes of elegance and comfort rather than castles.

the Christmas week of 1568 George, Earl of Shrewsbury, and his family, including guests, consumed three-quarters of wheat, 441 gallons of beer, 12 sheep, ten capons, 26 hens, seven pigs, six geese, seven cygnets, one turkey and 118 rabbits. Even if we assume a household of 100 or over it is a fairly hefty consumption. It has been estimated that beer consumption per person by day was between five and eight pints, in addition to wine. It is little wonder that foreigners were struck by the English fondness for drink!

Paternal Power in Aristocratic Families

In aristocratic families fathers continued to exercise almost dictatorial powers. It was common practice for children to kneel down before their father even in adult life. An extreme example of this was Sir Dudley North who, though in his sixties, 'would never put on his hat or sit down before his father enjoined him to it'. Such authoritarianism often produced tensions between children and their parents and it was said that often 'the child perfectly loathed the sight of his parents as the slave his torturer'. Perhaps the relationship between son and father, the respect given yet the hatred involved, is neatly illustrated by the story of Walter Raleigh and his son. Sir Walter Raleigh quarrelled with his son at the dinner table and:

> gives his son a damned blow over the face; his son, rude as he was, would not strike his father, but strikes over the face of the Gentleman that sate next to him, and sayed 'Box about 'twill come to my Father anon'.

The power exercised by the upper-class father was due largely to the children's economic dependence. The eldest son, who inherited the estates, could not marry until the allowance from his father was sufficient or his father died.

11 Sir Walter Raleigh. His relations with his eldest son seem typical of the tension that existed between father and son in the 17th century.

Younger sons had more freedom as they were expected to earn their own living as soldiers, merchants or lawyers. Daughters were in a worse position. Fathers felt obliged to marry off their daughters in this period, as there were no longer nunneries for the unmarried, and spinsters were frowned upon. 'There is nothing so ignominious as an overyeared maid, nor so much despised', wrote the diarist John Evelyn in the mid-seventeenth century. But a daughter's chance of marrying was almost entirely dependent on the size of the 'portion' (money provided by her father for the bridegroom), since marriage was essentially a financial arrangement, as a famous letter of William Cecil to his son Robert on what he should look for in his bride illustrates:

Let her not be too poor, how generous soever, for a man can buy nothing in the market with gentility. Nor choose a base and uncomely creature altogether for wealth, for it will cause contempt in others and loathing in thee. Neither make a choice of dwarf or fool, for by one thou shalt beget a race of pigmies, and the other will be thy continual disgrace . . .

Even more to the point, Thomas Osborne said that the future conjugal happiness could be calculated by the size of a wife's portion. By the seventeenth century upper-class women were in a vulnerable position in the marriage stakes, since there appear to have been considerably fewer men than women. A ballad entitled *The Wiving Age* is subtitled 'A great complaint of the Maidens of London, who now for the lacke of good Husbands are undone'.

Marriage among the Aristocracy

Men's attitudes to marriage tended to be far from romantic. Sir Charles Guise was frank about his motive for marriage: 'I was indebted above £2,000 so that I found myself in a manner enforced to look after another match'. The first Lord Guildford married because he fancied 'in the night human heat was friendly', which might at least be interpreted as showing a human rather than a financial interest! Sir Nicholas Poyntz was horrified to think that marriage had anything to do with romance: 'I am much troubled to think that I must speak to any woman one loving word'. Men could pick and choose their wives — or not marry. Sir Henry Lee 'never married but kept a woman to read to him while he was in bed'.

12   Lady Jane Grey. By her own account her upbringing was very severe and she never seems to have escaped from the power of her parents who helped persuade her to take the English throne. This action led to her execution.

Since marriages were still mainly arranged by parents it was possible for the wedding pair to be almost strangers on their wedding day, having only met for a few hours previously. Moreover though the common age for the upper classes to marry was between 20 and 25 there were plenty of examples of younger people marrying. In 1610 Lord Willoughby, just out of university, married Cassandra then 11 years old, the daughter of Sir Thomas Ridgeway. They were 'bedded' at 4 a.m. the morning after the wedding feast, and the next day Lord Willoughby went to France for four years. In 1695 the Duke of Bedford and his bride, with combined ages of 27, were scolded on their wedding day for running away from their reception to play in the garden.

The wedding ceremony was a great public occasion. After the blessing in the Church, there was a huge feast for guests to which all relatives and friends were invited. This frequently ended in the public bedding of the couple, who were led to their bedroom by the guests and then 'naked within the drawn curtains of the great four poster, the room still echoing with the parting drunken obscenities of the wedding guests, the two strangers were left to make each other's acquaintance'. Moreover if, in the early seventeenth century either the bride or the groom was a royal favourite, the couple had to stay in bed until King James came to question them on the first night of married life.

Though marriage remained essentially a financial arrangement and children were subject to strict parental control, greater freedom was emerging in the seventeenth century. Puritan preachers put great stress on the importance of the family as a Christian institution and condemned the practice of marrying merely for money. They condemned too the 'double standard' whereby husbands could take a mistress, but the wife was expected to remain faithful. Once extra-marital sex was condemned sons began to assert their right to choose their own partner. Attitudes began to change. Henry, Earl of Huntingdon, for example, said that he was against forced marriages:

> I myself was married when a child and could not have chosen so well myself nor been so happy in any woman I know, but because one proves well it must not beget a conclusion. [That is, the exception does not prove the rule].

James I declared that 'parents may forbid their children an unfit marriage but they may not force their consciences'.

Children of the Aristocracy

It would appear that aristocratic children were beginning to receive more affection in the seventeenth century. Certainly children were given more prominence in family portraits and the effigies of those who died young frequently appear

13   Holbein's drawing of Thomas More and his family. More, one of the great scholars of the 16th century, put great emphasis on family life. He had considered becoming a priest, but decided that the Christian ideal could be achieved equally well as a family man.

on tombs alongside their parents. There was an important change in child rearing in aristocratic families. In the sixteenth century all mothers sent their children to be fed by a woman in the neighbourhood who had recently had a baby (this was known as wet nursing) until the child was two or three. The reason for this practice was the belief that breast-feeding ruined the shape of the mother's breasts. But in the seventeenth century aristocratic mothers began to breastfeed their own children because it was felt that wet nursing led to weak children. For example Sir Hugh Cholmley complained that his weak and stunted frame was due to his being put onto a wet nurse with a poor supply of milk, though one wonders how he remembers such a point! In 1628 the Countess of Lincoln published a book urging mothers to feed their own children, and this book enjoyed considerable popularity. Many doctors today would argue that breastfeeding increases the emotional tie between mother and baby and this possibly played a part in developing more affectionate relationships between children and parents in the seventeenth century.

Non-Aristocratic Families

Outside the aristocracy pre-industrial households and families were not large. The largest household found in England in the seventeenth century outside the nobility was that of Richard Newdigate in Warwickshire. In 1684 he had a household of 37 which consisted of seven daughters under 16 years old and 28 servants. But this was the household of a rich landowner on the fringes of the aristocracy. The largest known family in seventeenth-century England was that of a pub owner in Harefield, Middlesex. He had 12 children aged between two and 22. The eldest two daughters had left home, but six more worked in the bar, in addition to an aunt. Needless to say there were no outside barmaids employed!

The average family however was much smaller, even when it included outsiders. A London baker's household in 1614 consisted of the baker and his wife, four paid employees called journeymen, two apprentices, two maidservants and four children. They all lived and worked in the same house. The baker was a boss to the journeymen who received 2s 6d (12½p) per week for working for him, but he was more like a father to the apprentices. They had to agree to stay with their master for seven years, and strict conditions were laid down on the apprentice:

> Taverns and ale houses he shall not haunt, dice, cards or any other unlawful game he shall not use, fornication with any woman he shall not commit, matrimony with any woman he shall not contract. He shall not absent himself by night or day without his master's leave but be a true and faithful servant.

14   The baking of bread: though many wives baked their own, bakeries were numerous, especially in towns. This was usually a family business involving husband, wife and children.

15 *opposite* On the farm there were always jobs for the whole family. There was no separation of home and work. Here all the men, women and children have a job to do.

> Food, drink, clothing, lodging and teaching in art, science or occupation with moderate correction.

The sons and the daughters probably worked in the bakery, at least part time, from an early age. John Locke the English philosopher writing at the end of the seventeenth century thought that children of farmers and tradesmen should start work at the age of three. In the bakery the children would help in the 'bolting', that is the sieving of the flour. Nevertheless the children received some schooling, as 6d (2½p) per week is allowed in the family budget for their school fees.

Poverty

In contrast to the extravagant living of upper-class families, that of tradesmen and farmers were modest. The baker's family had a total income of £6.50 per week for the entire household, out of which they spent just less than half on food. But such families were comfortably off, whereas labouring families always lived near the poverty line. Conditions were particularly bad in the sixteenth century due to inflation and unemployment. The results were stark, as a pamphlet of 1546 points out:

> Many thousands of us which here before lived honestly upon our sore labour and travayl (work) are now constrained some to begge, some to borrowe and some to robbe and steale to get food for us and our poor wives and children.

The practice of sending children away from home at an early age to become servants eased the burdens on poor families. Servants probably comprised some 10-15 per cent of England's population. But this practice was not always

successful. A good number of seventeenth-century prostitutes were girls who had run away from domestic service. Many girls, then as today, ran away to London, where they found grinding poverty. A girl called Joan Martindale came from Yorkshire to London in the 1640s and was so poor that she tried to sell her hair. But in general conditions improved somewhat for poor families in the second half of the seventeenth century. Nevertheless Gregory King, one of England's earliest statisticians, reckoned that of 1,360,000 families in England in 1688, some 400,000 were pauper families. John Locke wrote in 1696 that labourers lived on the breadline:

> for the labourers' share being seldom more than a bare subsistence, never allows that body of men time or opportunity to raise their thoughts above that.

The farmer's family, like that of the baker, was a working unit. The women kept the house and made butter and cheese. The boys and men did the ploughing, hedging and carting. Many people have seen this as a great family advantage, making for harmony and unity, but this working and living together also created tensions, especially as there was less leisure activity outside the home than today. The only outing for wives and daughters was the weekly church visit; husbands then, as now, frequented alehouses. Tensions in poor families were occasionally manifest in parents bringing down a formal curse upon their children — the reverse of the common practice of giving parental blessings. Such a curse was thought to have great effect:

> A parent curses his child and God says Amen to it. Hereupon the child is obsessed or strangely handled, peradventure perishes.

In 1665 a mother, one Rachael Dewsall of Hereford who disapproved of her son's marriage, burst into the wedding ceremony 'pulled up her clothes and kneeled down upon her bare knees and cursed her son and daughter (in law to be) and wished they might never prosper'.

16 Haymaking: a print from an early 17th-century ballad. Haymaking was traditionally a time for romance and haystacks traditionally the centre for frolicking. Here we see an affectionate couple in the hay.

17 This print from a 17th-century ballad shows a supper at an inn. Men tended to eat out much more than women in the 17th century, partly because they were more likely to be travelling, but also because a woman's place was still very much in the home.

More than the upper classes, ordinary men and women tried to keep the laws on marriage and sex laid down by society. But in some areas of England this did not mean a church wedding before the pair lived together. In Leicestershire the practice of 'handfasting' was common. Once a contract for a wedding had been agreed between the two sets of parents, the pair then set up house together. It was later, often when a child had been conceived, that a church wedding took place.

While living together before a church wedding was tolerated in some areas, couples were severly punished if they begot illegitimate children. In the seventeenth century the Lancashire Quarter Sessions record the following:

> Jane Sotworth of Wrightington, spinster, swears that Richard Garstange of Fazarkerly, husbandman, is the father of Alice her bastard daughter. She is to have charge of the child for two years provided she does not beg, and Richard is then to take charge until it is 12 years old. He shall give Jane a cow and 6s [30p] in money. Both he and she shall this day be whipped in Ormeskirke.

Since the unmarried mother had often to be maintained by the parish, illegitimacy was condemned on economic as well as moral grounds. Some unmarried mothers were so desperate that they murdered their children, and in 1623 Parliament passed 'an Act to prevent the murdering of Bastard Children'. The Act explains that some women, having given birth to a bastard:

> to avoid their shame and escape punishment do secretly bury or conceal the death of their children and after the child be found dead the said women do allege that the said child was born dead whereas sometimes the said child was murdered by the same lewd mothers.

It is impossible to know how widespread this infanticide was, but the fact that Parliament should legislate against it is in itself significant.

If the parents of an illegitimate child were unable to provide for it, the parish paid for the baby to be nursed. Such nurses were often well paid, receiving up to 5s (25p) per week. In general this practice seems to have worked well, but some women set up 'baby farms' and tried to make a business of it. An extreme example of abuse occurred in 1694 when one Mary Compton was found guilty of having starved and murdered several infants in her care, while she continued to draw 4-5s per week for each child.

The Family Life of Ralph Josselin

Ralph Josselin, who was born in 1620, was a puritan vicar in Earls Colne in Essex near Colchester. He kept a diary throughout his married life and we are able to see many details of himself and his family.

Ralph Josselin and his wife Jane had 'ten live born children in 21 years', though five of the children died before their parents. Jane also had at least five miscarriages. What is striking is the delight with which the pregnancies were recorded. Ralph talks of the 'great joy and comfort' when Jane became pregnant and he valued children 'above gold and jewels', partly for the pleasure they gave and partly for the comfort they would provide later — this despite the ghastliness of pregnancy and childbirth in the seventeenth century. In her fourth pregnancy Ralph records 'my wife faints and is pained with her child', and later 'my poore wife very ill, she breeds with difficulty'. Jane's last delivery at the age of 43 seems to have been the worst. 'My deare wife after many sad pains and sadder feares, in respect of the unkindliness of her labour was yett through God's mercy delivered of her tenth child.' It is interesting to note that Ralph appears to have been at the births — something we tend to think of as a very recent practice.

Much seventeenth-century literature stressed the authority of the father over his children, but Ralph Josselin's views, as reflected in one of his sermons, seem very liberal and modern:

> Now what have we received from our parents? We received from them our life under God and our bringing up and education, with a great deal of care and labour and with all love and tenderness. Now [you ought to] returne that love and tenderness to your parents with all willingness.

18 The alehouse had obvious attractions for men in the 18th century. Not only could they escape from a squalid home and the pressures of family, but also the serving maids were often friendly!

Certainly the children seem to have made their own choice in marriage partners. Ralph's own marriage was evidently a romantic and not an arranged one, and he describes how his 'eye fixed with love upon a Maid and hers upon me, who afterwards proved my wife'. He allowed his daughter Mary to turn down a suitor because he was 'not loving' and Ralph explained that he 'could not desire it' (the match) when she said it would make their lives miserable. It is only fair to add that Mary also rejected her suitor because he was not rich enough! Moreover Ralph's son John married without his parents' knowledge. 'John married unknown to me, God pardon his errors', wrote Ralph. To make matters worse Ralph disliked his daughter-in-law and added gloomily 'John's wife is likely to be a trouble to us'.

But John was obviously the black sheep of the family and Ralph records their turbulent relationship. 'John's debauchery in swearing sad' and 'John robed his mother and sister of neare 30s [£1.50] and away, God in his mercy break his heart for good', are typical entries in Ralph's diary. After the death of his elder brother, Thomas, John was the only surviving son and Ralph threatened to disinherit him more than once. But in the end he left him most of the estate and, throughout, Ralph gives the impression of being a loving, if exasperated father, rather than the heavy-handed puritan so often portrayed in seventeenth-century literature.

Ralph and his wife seem to have been affectionate to one another. 'In my absence she was wondrous sad and discontented', while, when he was ill: 'my deare wife (was) exceeding tender and careful of me'. They worked together on the farm which went with the vicarage and Ralph tells of 'when my wife and I pulling down a tree with a rope our pulling all fell together, but no hurt God be praised'. But there were considerable tensions also, especially when the children left home. At first Ralph recorded the joy of 'not a child at home but sensible of the comfort of my wife, my love, seeing everything more pleasant because I have her'. But thereafter we hear only complaints. Ralph got very incensed at his wife's failure to look after his ulcerated leg: 'my wife on some discontent which I know not would not assist mee in dressing my poor leg'.

What is striking about Ralph Josselin's family and family life is its similarity to the modern family. Ralph's relations with his wife and children were far from authoritarian. As Alan Macfarlane in his book, *The Family Life of Ralph Josselin,* says: 'if Josselin is a typical puritan, fathers were less austere, and less able to exert control of their children than some historians would have us believe'. Moreover Josselin's was very much the nuclear family; there were no relatives other than his children in close contact with the family and even the children left home early and often settled a considerable distance away. It might also be a comfort to modern fathers to know that a godly puritan minister had a son as troublesome as John Josselin!

3
The Impact of Industrialization on Working-Class Families

The Industrial Revolution, which began in Britain around 1780, affected the lives of many people more fundamentally than any other change in history. By the middle of the nineteenth century twice as many people worked in factories as on the land, and these factory workers lived in expanding towns. But life in the countryside also changed: indeed the agrarian revolution of the eighteenth century, which saw wide-scale enclosure and improved farming techniques, was a necessary forerunner of industrial development. Therefore families who moved to the new industrial areas and families who remained on the land both experienced dramatic changes by the mid-nineteenth century.

The Rural Family
The rural family was still a working unit in the eighteenth century. Wives and children were often engaged in some form of home-based textile production to eke out the proceeds from agriculture. In Westermorland and Cumberland farmers' wives spun their own wool and brought the yarn to market every week; on Welsh farms flannel was produced for the market and in wool-producing districts a few pieces of cloth were made and sold each year. Where goods were not produced for the market it was customary in the north in the mid-eighteenth century for women to produce a:

> coarse grey woollen cloth, made from a mixture of black and white wool for the clothing of the farmer and his family.

One or two Welsh sheep were kept to provide wool for stockings! As late as 1797 a contemporary could say of the north of England:

> almost every article of dress worn by the farmers, mechanics and labourers is manufactured at home; they are mainly respectable persons, at this day, who never wore a bought pair of stockings, coat nor waistcoat in their lives.

It was common custom on the death of a farmer who had no son, for his widow or daughters to take over the farm.

Even more important in the economy of many farms was dairy produce, and it was the women of the family who ran this. 'The woman who manages', says Mr Poyser in *Adam Bede*, 'has a large share in making the rent so that she may well be allowed to have her opinion on stock and their "keep" '. Wives and daughters would be concerned with the rearing and feeding of calves and pigs. Also the dairywoman often took her butter to the nearest retail market and was responsible for the sale of her cheese at the annual cheese fair.

Lower down the social scale the wives and daughters of the 'cottagers', whose husbands hired themselves out as day labourers, also contributed greatly to the family budget. Jane Millward from Shropshire had just over an acre of land on which she grew potatoes, wheat and garden produce. At first she depended on neighbouring farmers to plough the land for her, but since they always left her land until last, she decided to do the whole by hand, with a little help from her husband in taking up the crops. After 13 years her wheat crop was 'four times the general average', and she could provide her family with bread for more than half a year, in addition to the potatoes and vegetables she grew.

19 A painting by William Hogarth of a comfortable 18th-century family, the Cholmondleys. The children are dressed like adults, but they appear to be enjoying a certain amount of freedom. Their home life was not disrupted by the Industrial Revolution.

Prosperity for Some

But eighteenth-century developments in agriculture and industry changed family life in the countryside. The agrarian revolution brought considerable prosperity to many farmers. Farmers' wives and children ceased to work, and the females tried to emulate the gentility of the upper classes. Arthur Young, a writer on agriculture, mocked the tendency for:

> the ladies to be educated at expensive boarding schools, and the sons at the University, to be made parsons. . . all these things imply a departure from that line which separates these different orders of beings; let these things and all the folly, foppery, expense and anxiety that belongs to them, remain among gentlemen. A wise farmer will not envy them.
>
> (Ivy Pinchbeck, *Women Workers and the Industrial Revolution*)

The household also changed. Up to this time the farmer's family had lived in the great kitchen, sharing a table with the servants. But gradually the farmer's family moved to a small dining room for meals:

> opening into the kitchen with the glass in the door or the wall to see that things go right.

Poverty for Others

With the growth of factories the domestic system of textile production was gradually pushed out, and certainly by the 1830s at the latest homemade textiles could not compete with mass production. Rural families lost a valuable source of income. Moreover with the reorganization of agriculture, especially the enclosure of land in the second half of the eighteenth century, many cottages were pulled down, their gardens incorporated into newly-enlarged farms, and families crowded into old farmhouses without a scrap of garden where they might keep a pig or a chick.

Both these developments meant less work for women and children.

> Few of these are constantly employed except in harvest, so that the whole burden of providing for their families rests upon the man.

Moreover, the end of the eighteenth and the first half of the nineteenth century were years of severe economic hardship. The bad economic position of the rural family deprived of female and child income was chronic. 'An amazing number of people', wrote Davies in his book *The Case of Labourers in Husbandry*, 'have been reduced from a comfortable state of independence to the precarious position of mere hirelings, who when out of work come immediately to the parish'. In the south of England, where wages lagged behind the industrial north in the nineteenth century, the wives of farm labourers could not afford the fuel to cook a hot meal more than once or twice a week.

20 Certain working-class people such as this tailor's family still worked at home, even in the mid-19th century. The stark conditions revealed here suggest that home-based work was not necessarily more comfortable than factory life.

Housing Conditions

The housing conditions of the farm labourers varied enormously; in the Cotswolds and the West Riding of Yorkshire the buildings were of stone; in Lancashire and the Midlands of bricks. In other areas cottages were made of wattle and daub, and sometimes a half-timbered construction was used. William Blades, an East Riding agricultural worker who was born in 1839, probably lived in one of the better cottages:

> The house of the Blades family was, like all the houses of the agricultural labourers, small, consisting of two room on the ground floor called the 'house' or living room and the parlour, with two bedrooms above. In many of the cottages at that time there was over one or other of the sleeping chambers a space or area . . . which went by the name of 'cockloft'.
>
> (J.F.C. Harrison, *The Early Victorians 1832-51*)

By contrast, as late as early this century, charcoal burners and their families still lived in small huts built with turf and sacking over a pole frame. A charcoal burner's camp has been reconstructed at the Weald and Downland Open Air Museum at Singleton in Sussex. This shows that a large hut was used to provide a living room for the family, while smaller ones, each with two beds, served as bedrooms.

The Family Unit Maintained

Despite the general changes described, family life remained virtually unchanged in some areas and the family continued as an economic unit. The nineteenth-century novelist Mrs Gaskell notes the northern hill farmers as:

> just, independent, upright. . . disliking change and new ways and new people; sensible and shrewd, each household self-contained.

Another contemporary commentary said of the hills above Fylde in Lancashire:

> many families have lived on the same farm for generations; and by frequent intermarriage they have become connected together almost like one family.

In the more backward economic regions women continued to do the most burdensome of the farm jobs. In 1823 Hugh Miller, a Scottish journalist, described farming in the Highlands:

> There is neither horse nor plough in the village — a long, crook-handled kind of spade, termed a cass-chrom, and the hoe, supplying the place of the latter — the Highlander himself, and more particularly his wife, that of the former (i.e. they do the work of the horse) — for here (shall I venture the expression?) as in all semi-barbarous countries, the woman seems to be regarded rather as the drudge than the companion of man. It is the part of the husband to turn up the land and sow it, the wife conveys the manure to it in a square creel (with a slip bottom), tends the corn, reaps it, hoes the potatoes, digs them up, and carries the whole home on her back. (Peter Bayne, ed., *The Life and Letters of Hugh Miller*, 2 vols, 1871, Vol 1 p.115.)

In the more remote and conservative agricultural communities parents were able to control their childrens' marriages both in the timing and choice of partner. But generally we know little about the personal details surrounding courtship and marriage in rural families. Historians need perhaps to explore oral traditions as well as documents: they might find more stories such as that of Charles Andrews, an asparagus seller of Willersey, Gloucestershire. Charlie was in lodgings, where his landlady was living with a man who was not her husband, and who frequently beat her when he was drunk. Charlie took pity on his landlady and proposed marriage, though she was 30 years older than he. They went to live in Willersey and when the old woman died at the age of 90 Charlie was sad: 'She has been like a mother to me'.

21 With the Industrial Revolution women increasingly had the opportunity to go out and work in the factories. Some have seen this as an emancipating step for women, but much of the work was regimented and monotonous, as we can see from this button factory.

Working Mothers

In contrast to developments in the countryside, the Industrial Revolution increased employment for women and children, at least until the middle of the nineteenth century. Engels, the friend of Karl Marx, considered that this ruined the family. 'When women work in factories', he wrote, 'the most important result is the dissolution of family ties'. Other critics argued that mothers neglected their children, while the father lost his authority in the family since he was supported financially by his wife and children. Moreover the family suffered from appalling living and working conditions. But above all, so nineteenth-century critics maintained, the family was undermined by increased sexual immorality resulting from women going into factories and mines. Conversely some nineteenth-century writers and modern historians have claimed that though the family changed considerably, it emerged just as strong as it ever was at the end of the nineteenth century.

Critics of the factory system aimed to show that the working mother ruined her family. Lord Ashley, a great advocate of factory reform, predicted pessimistically that:

domestic life and discipline must soon be at an end; society will consist of individuals no longer grouped into families, so early is the separation of husband and wife, of parents and children.

P. Gaskell, in his book *Artisans and Machinery: the Moral and Physical Conditions of the Manufacturing Population* (1836), was even more gloomy. Family life consisted of:

parental cruelty and carelessness, filial disobedience, neglect of conjugal rights, absence of maternal love, destruction of brotherly and sisterly affection are too often its constituents and the results of such a combination are moral degradation, ruin of domestic enjoyments and social misery.

(H. Perkin, *The Origins of Modern English Society*)

22 Drink was a common cause of financial and physical ruin. Cruikshank's grotesque cartoon of the Gin Shop shows Death waiting for his next victims.

But such a view is by no means supported by the factory workers themselves. A witness before the 1833 Factory Commission denied that factory girls made bad wives:

I have heard it said so, but I know to the contrary because I married three wives out of the factory, and I take that as proof. I am certain that as good wives may be had from the factories as from any other occupation.
(H. Perkin, *The Origins of Modern English Society*)

In fact it seems fairly certain that relatively few *mothers* worked in the factories; women tended then as now to leave work when they had children. A contemporary wrote of Nottingham in the mid-nineteenth century:

It is rare to find a mother who has a couple of children alive working in a mill. The duties of domestic life compel her to stay at home.

Henry Ashworth, a model cotton employer of Egerton and Turton declared that he employed no married women and that his workmen did not want their wives to work. Even Engels who was so critical of the factory system admitted that in 412 Manchester factories less than 20 per cent of the female work force was married.

But it has been shown that infant mortality was higher in families with working mothers, whether in the factories or in the fields. During the cotton famine of the 1860s, for example, when many women were out of work, the infant mortality rate in Lancashire actually fell, despite the fact that families were poorer. This proves the importance of maternal care. One historian has written of the horrors of 'day nursing by amateur baby minders, "infants preservatives" containing narcotics to keep her charges quiet'. But in a recent book, *Family Structure in Nineteenth Century Lancashire*, Michael Anderson found that only 20 per cent of all infant children in industrial Lancashire were left with professional childminders: children were generally looked after by the grandmother or a close friend. But in the unhygienic conditions of nineteenth-century urban life, breastfeeding probably assumed a special importance, and the factory mother could not breastfeed her child. A feeding bottle of the period, with a leather teat, looks most unhygienic.

The Woman's Changing Role

A great concern of many factory critics seems to have been that the authority of the father in the family was being diminished because his wife and daughters were earning money. A popular misconception was that wives often kept their unemployed or idle husbands. But a survey of Deansgate in Manchester in 1865 showed that less than 2 per cent of the families there were maintained by the wife's wage. Nevertheless Lord Ashley was certain that:

> females not only perform the labour but occupy the places of men (in the mill towns). They are forming various clubs and associations and gradually acquiring all those privileges which are held to be the proper portion of the male sex.

In such clubs females get together to drink, sing and smoke, and they use the 'most brutal and disgusting language imaginable'. Lord Ashley then related a dialogue which he claimed was told to him by an eyewitness.

> A man came into one of those clubs with a child in his arms. 'Come lass', said he, addressing one of the women. 'Come home, for I cannot keep this bairn quiet and the others I have left crying at home.' 'I won't come home, idle devil', she replied. 'This is but the second pint (of ale) that me and Bess have had between us. If I have the labour I will also have the amusement'.

I think it is fair to say that Lord Ashley exaggerated the effects of the factory system.

But it seems likely that the Industrial Revolution gave women greater freedom and authority in the family. The Handloom Weavers' Commission of 1840 argued that the cotton girls were independent compared to the daughters of the middle class.

A young woman prudent and careful, and living with her parents, from the age of 16 to 25 may in that time, by factory employment, save £100 as a wedding portion. I believe it to be to the interest of the community that every young woman should have this in her power. She is not driven into an early marriage by the necessity of seeking a home; and a consciousness of independence in being able to earn her own living is favourable to the development of her best moral energies.

(H. Perkin, *The Origins of Modern English Society*)

Perhaps the mother's position in the family was enhanced by her dual role within the home and as a wage earner outside. This could also mean of course, the worst of both worlds:

At weekends the men and the single women really make holiday. . . the married women who seem the slaves of Lancashire society, are then obliged to set to work harder than ever to do shopping and housework.

In the working-class industrial family it was the wife who controlled the family finances. This was probably also so in labouring families in the country, but contrasts with the male-dominated middle-class family. It was the wife who had to make ends meet in times of economic hardship. Some contemporary comment was full of praise for such wives.

I have sometimes thought that a family undergoing such a trial (i.e. unemployment) is like a crew at sea short of provisions . . . there it is the wife who is captain, she is the provider and distributor. The husband under such circumstances leaves all to her, and right nobly does she discharge her post.

23 A number of working-class families were incapable of looking after their children because they were too poor. Such children had to rely on charity.

Family Relationships

There is much evidence to suggest that far from breaking up, some working-class families were, despite enormous problems, closely knit and loving. An agent of the Liverpool District Provident Society commented that 'nothing can be more warm and keen than the affection of parents throughout the cotton district for children'. Moreover it was not lack of concern but economic necessity which forced parents to send their children into the factories. 'I could not support my children except they were to bring something in', said one handloom weaver in the 1840s. Even more telling was the case of the spinner who sent his first four children out into the mill at an early age, but kept the fifth child out until the age of 13 'because our circumstances were better'. Mothers went to work in the factories out of financial necessity, not because they cared little for their children. Even in the more prosperous years towards the end of the nineteenth century a factory inspectress found that of the working wives in the Potteries only in 18 per cent of cases was there no financial necessity for them to work.

Relations between mothers and children seem to have been particularly close, and mothers sometimes protected children from brutal fathers. A number of husbands were violent, drink being the main cause. A typical case was that of a London wife who complained:

> sometimes he ill-treats me. If he don't with his hand I know he does with his tongue. He has the most dreadful tongue ever heard of: he often drinks very hard. He's drunk whenever he has the money to be so. . . I'm ready to run away, and leave him very often. If it wasn't for my children I should do so.

Factors Adversely Affecting the Family

Drinking seems to have been a major social problem, and doubtless it put a great strain on many families. Manchester had nearly 1,000 pubs in the 1830s and Glasgow had one public house to every ten houses in 1840, and it was estimated that some 30,000 persons were drunk every Saturday night. Irishmen in the large towns operated illicit stills which added to the consumption of alcohol. Drinking was built into the very fabric of working-class life. Some groups such as the miners rightly claimed their need for drink:

> The thirst produced by our work is very excessive, it is completely as if you had a fever upon you. You can scrape the coal dust off the tongue with the teeth; and do what you will it is impossible to get the least spittle into the mouth.

There were a variety of customs which encouraged drinking. The plumbers forced an apprentice to buy a round of drinks when he cut his first sheet of lead. In the mills a change of shift was the occasion for a drink, and the first time a young man was seen by his mates with a woman (the 'bull shilling') provided another good reason for drinking.

Many critics of the factory system argued that increased sexual immorality of the industrial workers was destroying the family. A witness to the Factory Commission of 1833 said that it would be:

> no strain on his conscience to say that three quarters of the girls between 14 and 20 were unchaste.

P. Gaskell, always ready to denounce, added:

> The chastity of marriage is but little known among them; husband and wife sin equally, and a habitual indifference to sexual rights is generated which adds one other item to the destruction of domestic habits.
>
> (H. Perkin, *The Origins of Modern English Society*)

The close proximity of men and women in factories and mines was bound to lead to sexual relationships, so it was claimed. But some contemporaries argued that this was not the case. W. Cook Taylor, in his book *Factories and the Factory System* investigated the problem and concluded that:

> the returns show that seductions are of a rare occurrence (in factories) and that they usually take place in the evenings after work when they do occur, and that in nine cases out of ten the seducers do not belong to the same mill as the seduced.

Moreover, like the Leicestershire labourers in the seventeenth century, most of these couples intended to marry, though only when there was a child on the way. The 1833 Factory Commission finally concluded that:

> there is no evidence to show that vice and immorality are more prevalent among these people (factory workers) than other portions of the community in the same station.
>
> (H. Perkin, *The Origins of Modern English Society*)

In fact it has been shown that illegitimacy was less frequent in Lancashire than in Cumberland and Norfolk, where factory work for women scarcely existed. The charge that mills and coal mines encouraged sexual immorality seems totally unfounded.

Poor or even appalling housing was one of the main dangers to the well being of the family. Working-class housing in the towns varied almost as much as labourers' housing in the country. Skilled artisans had two-bedroomed cottages in the better areas of town, with a small back yard attached. But the cheaper houses were:

> built back to back with no possibility of good ventilation, and contain a

cellar for coals and food, the coal department being frequently tenanted by fowls, pigeons or rabbits, and in some cases with two or all three of these.

The interior consisted of 'a room from nine to 14 feet by from ten to 12 or 14 feet, to do all the cooking, washing and the necessary work of a family and another of the same size for all to sleep in. . . .' Worse still were the conditions in which the very poorest (often Irish immigrants) lived, in cities such as Manchester, Liverpool, Glasgow, London and Leeds. Robert Baker, a surgeon and factory inspector of Leeds, described these cellar dwellings:

I have been in one of these damp cellars without the slightest drainage, every drop of wet and every morsel of dirt and filth having to be carried up to the street; two corded frames for beds, overlaid with sacks for five persons. . . the floor in many places absolutely wet; a pig in the corner also; and in a street where filth of all kinds has accumulated for years.

The effect of urban living can be seen from statistics published by the Manchester Statistical Society in 1937, comparing the death rates of Manchester and Rutland among different classes.

Classes	Average Age of Death	
	Manchester	Rutland
Professional families	38	52
Tradesmen and their families	20	41
Mechanics, labourers and their families	17	38

24   Grinding poverty was a common feature of working class life in the 18th and 19th centuries. This Punch cartoon shows a matchmaker's family in despair because they are unable to pay their weekly rent.

25 *opposite*   Lodging houses for poor families in late 19th century London. Today we might think of the hazards of four-storey housing for families with young children, but their good construction and cleanliness made them models of their day.

26 'A Watery Nest' by Barnard. Even in the late 19th century the poorest families still lived in hovels like this.

27   A family of five living in one room in the 1880s.

Thus the lowest-class family in Rutland had a life expectancy equal to that of the Manchester professional classes. In the Manchester slums, the labourer and his family on average lived less than half the years of the Rutland labourer, and the very high level of infant mortality accounted for this incredibly low level of 17 years' life expectancy.

Conclusions

It is enormously difficult to generalise about the way the Industrial Revolution affected the standard of living of the working-class family. Skilled workers were usually in work and well paid, but casual labourers received lower wages and were frequently out of work. The standards varied yearly according to the state of the local and national economy. For example at the Styal Mill nine miles south of Manchester there was a mill shop whose accounts show that in a boom year of 1825 the girls bought hats and shoes instead of the traditional clogs and shawls. The boom in hats did not last long, for declining trade checked it and in 1826 only £10 was spent on them compared to £21 7s 3d (£21.36) a year earlier. Expenditure on food likewise depended on the fluctuations of trade, as Engels pointed out:

> The normal diet of the individual worker naturally varies according to his wages. The better-paid workers, particularly when the whole family works in the factories, enjoy food as long as they are in employment. They have meat every day and bacon and cheese for the evening meal. The lower paid workers have meat only two or three times a week and sometimes only on Sundays. The poorer workers can afford no meat at all and they eat bread, cheese, porridge and potatoes.

During the depression of the 1830s and 1840s, food consumption went down, and only after 1850 did the standard of living improve.

By the middle of the nineteenth century the town labourer's family was different from its equivalent 100 years earlier; but the family was not destroyed by industrialization, rather it adapted to its profound changes. This appears to be true of workers in the cotton industry at least, and the ability of the family to adapt to change may have been due to the gradual stages by which such change took place. Some of the earliest factories were still in the country and the family was kept together. Samuel Grey who owned the mill at Styal, mentioned above, built cottages for the families of his workers. As the workforce increased, a farm was bought which supplied the community with milk, butter and other dairy produce. By 1822 a chapel had been built, as many of the operatives were Baptists. Moreover in the early nineteenth century all members of one family might be employed together. The husbands did the highly-skilled job of spinning, while the wives and children worked as pickers, piecers or scavengers. But by the 1820s when the spinning process had become more mechanized, more labour was needed to support the spinner than could be had from his own family. This led to the employment of children without their parents.

By the 1830s therefore, we can speak of the break up of the old family. Increasingly a man, his wife and his children might all be performing different tasks in the factory and working different hours. Moreover children were often treated brutally. In the 1840s, Lancashire and Yorkshire Poor Law Guardians were sending paupers to the mines at the ages of six, seven and eight. One boy in Halifax was beaten by his master and had coals thrown at him, so he ran away. The boy said he fed on 'the candles that I found in the pits that the colliers left overnight'. An 18-year old girl, employed for 13 hours a day to open and close traps, complained: 'I have to trap without a light, and I'm scared . . . sometimes I sing when I've light, but not in the dark. I dare not sing then'.

Despite such pressures the family was not destroyed, but it did change its functions. By the end of the nineteenth century child labour had been greatly reduced. The amount of schooling received by working-class children correspondingly increased, especially after the 1870 Education Act. Whereas before the Industrial Revolution the home had been a place for work and whatever learning there was for children, it was now a place mainly for leisure. It is obvious that such a development had certain advantages as well as severe drawbacks.

28 Lord Shaftesbury, who was responsible for much reforming legislation including the prohibiting of the employment of women and children in the mines in 1842.

29 A cartoon by Cruikshank of a Ragged School. The 19th century saw the provision of schooling for working class families, but the emphasis was on cheapness, and standards were low.

4
The Victorian Family

The Industrial Revolution created a new middle class which brought new values to the family. In this new middle-class family parents, and in particular the father, were still distant from their children. The practice of employing a governess to teach children in their early years, the use of wet nurses and the fear of the authoritarian father, all contributed to this separation of parents

30 A very comfortable, elegant, 19th-century house in Clapham, London, built for the new wealthy upper-middle classes.

and children. Moreover the father was now absent from the home throughout the day, and the movement of the middle classes to the suburbs meant that the main meal was shifted from midday to the evening — often after the children had gone to bed. Other factors influenced the family in the nineteenth century. By the end of the century the size of the family was being limited, and even more significantly the role of women in the family and society at large was undergoing change. Indeed economic and social developments brought about a change in the very idea of the family.

The Aristocracy

Despite all these changes, however, the aristocratic family and household continued in its former style. The importance of the family was still emphasized by the elaborate celebrations of birth and marriage; in Alnwick Castle in Northumberland, for example, guns were fired in celebration of the birth of an heir. In 1845 when the Marquis of Worcester, son and heir of the Duke of Beaufort, came of age, 200 tenants were feasted in the servants' hall and celebrations lasted for a week.

31 Substantial terraced houses at Hornsey built for the artisan or lower-middle classes. These houses were well built and are valuable today.

32 A royal family party at Osborne House in the 1890s. Queen Victoria's emphasis on family symbolised the tremendous importance of the family for the Victorian middle classes.

33 What we think of as a typical upper-class Victorian family — elegantly dressed, confident, but showing few signs of enjoyment!

A large number of servants was still an essential part of the aristocratic household. Even in the 1890s the Duke of Westminster employed over 300 servants including ground staff at Eaton in Cheshire. In 1900 the Duke of Portland had a staff of 320 including over 50 servants in the kitchens at Welbeck Abbey. Here life seems to have changed little since the Middle Ages as one of the servants recalls:

The estate of Welbeck Abbey was more like a principality than anything else; there were scores of people working beside me whom I did not know. . . . within the borders of Welbeck Abbey His Grace the Duke of Portland wielded an almost feudal indisputable power.

The household was strictly hierarchical with the lesser servants under the control of the head servants.

Only the head servants and those in attendance on the sitting room or dining room would be likely even to know their employers by sight.

But there were certain rituals which emphasized the unity of the household and stressed the 'family' relationship. At Longleat every Christmas there was a grand ball for servants in the dining hall to which local tradesmen were invited. The ball was opened by the Marquis of Bath partnering the housekeeper while the Marchioness danced with the household steward. Another Christmas custom was that all the undermaids received a dress from Lady Bath, and on Christmas night, however cold, the maids danced in the courtyard watched by the gentry.

The Father's Role

The middle-class family tried to emulate the aristocracy but it was formed by new economic circumstances. The authority of the father had always been great but never more so than in the nineteenth-century middle-class family. The father was entirely responsible for the status of the family which was decided by his income alone. It was through the father's hard work that his children could be educated at the best fee-paying schools which would ensure their social status for the future.

34   A photograph of a family lower down the social scale, perhaps a farmer's family.

35   The heavy symbolism in this painting by Augustus Egg of the collapse of the house of cards, and the shipwreck and Expulsion from Paradise in the wall-picture, underlines the tragedy that has befallen the family. The husband confronts his wife with evidence of her adultery. Her pleading is to no avail; she will be expelled, penniless, from the home.

It was perhaps because of this that fathers had dictatorial rights over their children to the exclusion of the mother. In the early nineteenth century a father's right over the custody of the children was absolute. At common law a mother had no rights: even after the father's death the father's guardian took precedence over the mother. The defencelessness of the mother was brought out by a celebrated law case of the time. Caroline Norton left her husband and took with her the three children. Only then did she realize that in law she had no rights at all and that she might never again see her children unless her husband permitted it. She wrote of the suffering this brought.

What I suffered respecting those children God knows and He only. . . I believe men have no more notion of what that anguish is than the blind have of colours . . . I really lost my young children, craved for them, struggled for them, was barred from them — and came too late to see one that had died — except for his coffin.

It was not until 1928 that mothers achieved equal rights over their children.

The Wife's Role

In the early nineteenth century the wife was totally subordinate to her husband. Her duty was to love, honour and obey and indeed amuse her lord and master. The wife existed to manage the household and bring up his children. But there was a reverse side to the submissive Victorian wife; increasingly she was seen as a superior moral force who could 'improve' her husband. A wife should be 'a companion who will raise the tone of his (her husband's) mind from low anxieties and vulgar force'. The woman was the moral force not only in the family but in society as a whole. 'The only hope of society is in women', wrote Edwin Hood, 'the hope of the age is in women. On her depends mainly the righting of wrongs, the correcting of sins and the success of all missions'.

Victorian thinking about sex also tended to elevate the status of women within the family, though in a very narrow way. Reaction against the sexual laxity of the eighteenth century and the religious revival known as the Evangelical Movement, resulted in a tremendous emphasis on the virtue of chastity. According to most Victorian writers the purest women in the world was Mother. Many a Victorian son was told by his father 'Remember your dear good mother and never do anything she would be ashamed of'.

Closer Home Ties

Under the impact of the Industrial Revolution and the development of the commercial world the family and the home achieved a new significance. The home was a refuge from the toils of industry and business. The socialist writer Ruskin wrote in lyrical terms of the home:

> This is the true nature of the home, that it is the place of Peace; the shelter, not only from all injury but from all terror, doubt and division. Insofar as it is a sacred place, a vestal temple, a temple of the hearth watched over by the Household Gods, it vindicates the name and fulfils the praise of Home.

This highly sentimental picture of the Victorian home is reflected in Fanny Kingsley's account of family life on Sunday:

> There was always the Sunday walk, a stroll on the moor, and some fresh object of natural beauty pointed out at every step. Indoors the Sunday picture books were brought out. Each child had its own and chose subjects for father to draw, either some Bible story or bird or beast or flower mentioned in the Scripture. Happy Sundays! — never associated with gloom or restrictions but with God's work.

The Victorians certainly idealized the family, but evidence suggests that family ties were indeed becoming closer. Despite the great stress on financial matters there seems to be more consideration given to marrying for love, at least as reflected in the literature of the perod. In *Jane Eyre* the heroine, for all her admiration of St. John Rivers and her wish to work with him as a foreign missionary, refuses to marry him because they:

> did not love each other as a man and wife should. Can I receive from him the bridal ring, endure all forms of love and know that the spirit was absent? No: such a martyrdom would be monstrous.

By the middle of the nineteenth century a profound change had occurred in male attitudes towards the home and the relationship of husband and wife, according to the philosopher J.S. Mill. Writing in 1869 he argued that:

> the association of men and women in daily life is much closer and more complete than it was ever before. Man's life is more domestic. Formerly their pleasures and chosen occupations were among men and men's company; their wives had not a fragment of their lives. At the present time the turn of opinion against rough amusements and convivial exercises which formerly occupied most men in their hours of relaxation. . . have thrown the man very much on home and inmates for his personal and social pleasures.

The middle classes were enormously preoccupied with having the necessary money to live a family life of style. There could be no question of marrying unless the man had a certain level of income or capital. A pamphlet entitled *Economy for the Single and Married* was very pessimistic about those who received only £100 a year. It advised gloomily:

> steel yourself against the tender passion — for marry you cannot, with any propriety or hope of providing for a family. If however you *must* fall in love, use every effort to better your situation and await 'a proper time to marry'.

The average age at which middle-class men married in the mid-nineteenth century was almost 30 — a major cause of prostitution according to the *Times*.

The importance of money when considering family life was brought out in the *Times* correspondence in 1858 about whether it was possible for the middle classes to marry on £300 a year. It was considered to be a very doubtful proposition:

> Fancy the derisive outbursts you would excite at the club by asserting that 'young Jones with his £300 a year might marry and be happy!' Why that magnificent amount hardly suffices to keep him going.

But a London clerk replied that he was 'earning £250 a year and living six miles out in the suburbs in a small house with three bedrooms and a servant's room'. However he admitted that the one servant was only occasional and that he drank wine only once every five weeks. The *Times'* editorial commented rather gloomily that 'five years hence, if his family continues to increase a reduction of these comforts may be necessary'. The figure of £300 was, therefore, regarded as a minimum family income to maintain a middle-class life style. Anthony Trollope the novelist felt secure only when his income reached £14,000. Only now, he said, 'can I keep a good house over my head, insure my life, educate my two children and hunt perhaps twice a week'.

An adequate income was needed to acquire a home of suitable size and location. A clerk might be satisfied with three bedrooms, but for those with a number of servants, ten rooms or more was a minimum. But for those on the highest income a house such as Mr Pickwick's at Dulwich might be the ideal:

> Everything was so beautiful! The lawn in front, the garden behind, the miniature conservatory, the dining room, the drawing room, the bedrooms, the smoking room — and above all the study with its pictures and easy chairs. Everything was so beautiful, so compact and so neat, and in such exquisite taste, that there was no deciding what to admire most.

36 This is typical of many late Victorian posters: the advertisers were already directing their attention to the family.

37 From the *Book of Household Management* by Mrs Isabella Beeton in 1891. It would be interesting to compare this with modern prices, remembering that the list is in old pence.

The furnishing of houses could involve considerable expense. J.R. Walsh in his book *A Manual of Domestic Economy Suited to Families Spending from £100 to £1000 a Year,* published in 1857, said that a family could furnish a house consisting of a hall, kitchen, dining room, drawing room, library (or breakfast room) three bedrooms, two servants' rooms and a nursery, for £585. Some of the cheap warehouses in London, however, offered to furnish a ten bedroomed house for as little as £289. Outlay on furniture, therefore, was anything between half and a full year's annual income.

From the various magazines on good housekeeping we can see how the middle-class family spent its money. The author of *A New System of Practical Domestic Economy*, published in 1823, claimed that those with over £1000 a year should aim for the monthly expenditure listed on page 56.

59.—PROVISIONS AND HOUSEHOLD REQUISITES.

For Groceries, Tinned Provisions, Jams, Biscuits, and other household requisites, the prices quoted will be found a fair average of those charged by the principal provision dealers and grocers in London and the chief provincial towns.

Tinned Meats, Soups, Fish, Poultry, Fruit and Vegetables now occupy an important place in our food supply, being available at any time, and handy substitutes when fresh provisions may be difficult to procure. Under each division of our receipts will be found some giving full directions for their use.

GROCERY.

ARTICLE.	AVERAGE PRICE.	ARTICLE.	AVERAGE PRICE.
Almonds :—Jordan	2s. 6d. per lb.	Fruit—*continued.*	
Valencia	1s. per lb.	Greengages	1s. 4d. per lb.
Baking Powder	4½d. per pkt.	Chinois	1s. 4d. per lb.
Yeatman's Yeast	4½d. per pkt.	Cherries	1s. 3d. per lb.
Beef Essences (Brand's)	1s. 1½d. per tin.	Pears	1s. 4d. per lb.
Mason's	1s. 1½d. per tin.	Angelica	1s. 1d. per lb.
Liebig's	2s. 3d. per ¼ lb.	Figs	1s. 1d. per lb.
Beef Tea (Mason's)	1s. per skin.	Mixed	1s. 4d. per lb.
Blanc-mange Powder	10d. per tin.	Flour :—Best Whites	1s. 3d. 7 lbs. bag.
Capers (Harvest's)	7d. per bottle.	Self-raising	1s.10d. 12 lbs. bag.
Candied Peel :—Lemon	6d. per lb.	Whole Meal	1s. 5d. 7 lbs. bag.
Orange	7d. per lb.	Gelatine	3½d. per pkt.
Citron	9½d. per lb.	Ginger :—Cochin	10d. per lb.
Mixed	8d. per lb.	Ground	9d. per lb.
Chicory	4d. per lb.	Crystallised	1s. 1d. per lb.
Chocolate (Fry's)	10½d. per lb.	Preserved	9½d. small jar.
Best (Fry's)	11d. per tin.	Golden Syrup	11d. per 4 lb. tin.
Milk Paste	11d. per tin.	Herbs	5d. per bottle.
Tablets	1s. 10d. per pkt.	Isinglass	10½d. per pkt.
Cocoa (Cadbury's)	10½d. per lb.	Mustard	1s. 4d. 1 lb. tin.
Essence ,,	11d. per pkt.	Prunes	4d. per lb.
Nibs	1s. 3d. per lb.	Pudding Powder	6d. per pkt.
Cocoatina (Schweitzer's)	1s. 3d. per tin.	Raisins :—	
Coffee : French	1s. 4d. per lb.	Valencia	5½d. per lb.
East India	1s. 5d. per lb.	Sultanas	4½d. per lb.
Mocha	1s. 6½d. per lb.	Muscatels	1s. 4d. per lb.
Coffee and Milk	9½d. per tin.	Spices, various	4½d. per tin.
Currants	4d. per lb.	Sugar :—Demerara	2½d. per lb.
Custard Powder	4½d. per tin.	Loaf	2½d. per lb.
Curry Powder	1s. 6d. per bottle.	Tea :—Congou	2s. per lb.
Paste	1s. 2d. per jar.	Ceylon	2s. 4d. per lb.
Egg Powder (Harvest's)	6d. per pkt.	Orange Pekoe	2s. 8d. per lb.
Fruit, Crystallised :		Gunpowder	3s. per lb.
Apricots	1s. 6d. per lb.	Assam Pekoe	6d. per tin.
Almonds	1s. 1d. per lb.	Oolong	2s. 6d. per lb.
Lunettes	1s. 2d. per lb.	Young Hyson	3s. per lb.
Melon	1s. 6d. per lb.	Consolidated	2s. 8d. per lb.
Mixed	1s. 4d. per lb.	Yeast Powder	2s. 8d per lb.

	1	*Household Expenses*			
		Provisions	£26		
		Coals	£ 7		
		Extra for Entertainment	£ 2		
		Medicine	£ 1		Total — £36
	2	Houses and Carriages	£10		
		Male servants	£ 8		
		Female servants	£ 4		Total — £22
	3	*Clothes etc.*			
		Gentleman's clothes	£ 4		
		Lady's clothes	£ 5		
		Three children	£ 2	10s	
		Haberdashery		10s	Total — £12
	4	*Rent, Taxes, Repairs*			
		Rents	£ 8		
		Taxes and Repairs	£ 4		Total — £12
	5	*Extra Expenses*			
		Education	£ 4		
		Pocket Expenses	£ 2		
		Private Expenses	£ 2		Total — £8
	6	Reserve or Saving	£10		Total — £10
					£100

This expenditure was geared to the average-sized middle-class family of three or four children, plus a number of servants.

Rising Costs

In the 1870s there were numerous complaints of the increased cost of living for the middle-class family: 'It is a universal complaint the substantial truth of which cannot be denied' wrote R.W. Greg in 1875, 'that life to a vast proportion of the middle classes is becoming more difficult and costly'. He concluded that 'on the whole we are within the mark if we say that among the average middle class families the actual cost of living is 25 per cent higher than it was 25 years ago'.

The increased cost of living for middle-class families was due, however, more to 'keeping up appearances' as a contemporary put it in 1873, than to increases in food prices or servants' wages. Greg admitted that middle-class families invariably kept up with fashion.

However resolute to live as we think we ought, and not as others around us, it is, as we shall find, simply *impossible* not to be influenced by their example and to fall into their ways unless we are content either to live in remote districts or in an isolated fashion.

One such source of increased expenditure was the habit of dining well. 'Gentlemen must have their sumptuous dinners well served and expensive wines or they raise the cry that they have nothing to eat', wrote a correspondent in *Quarterly Review of Social Science* in 1861. The average consumption of wine more than doubled in the 20 years following 1860. In the years 1850-75 prices rose by only 5 per cent, but improvements in the style of life of the middle-class family necessitated an extra expenditure of 50 per cent if status was to be maintained.

Servants

Essential to the status of the middle class was the keeping of domestic servants. Seebohm Rowntree took 'the keeping or not keeping of domestic servants as the dividing line between the working classes and those of a higher social scale'. A large number of servants was an indication of social superiority and some Victorian hosts placed their guests at the table according to the number of servants they kept.

Only the richer homes would have a butler who received a high salary and whose duty 'included such an acquaintance with the wine trade as would fit him to conduct the business of a wine merchant'. But the average middle-class family probably had three servants — cook, parlourmaid and housemaid — all female, as women were cheaper to hire. 'The parlourmaid's work is the same as the work undertaken in grander establishments by the butler and his assistants; she has the care of plate and glass and the place she works is always called the pantry', explained Booth and Argyle in *Life and Labour of the People of London* (1896).

The second half of the nineteenth century was the peak period for the employment of domestic servants. By 1871 some 12.8 of the female population was in service or allied occupations, though male labour was becoming

38 Three different kinds of feeding bottle used in the Victorian period, made of glass, pewter and pottery.

too expensive. With increased opportunities for women in the last quarter of the nineteenth century the number of servants dropped, but up to the end of the century numbers remained high and the wages of domestics increased by up to 30 per cent in the last quarter of the century.

Many a Victorian home was entirely geared to servants. The Rector of Odell in Bedfordshire in the 1890s kept seven servants. But there were ten children to be looked after (well above the average!) and a variety of household chores.

There must have been at least 15 oil lamps to fill and trim daily. A gardener and coachman were also employed and their daily work consisted in pumping water to the house twice a day.[There were] at least 15 pairs of boots to clean daily. On Monday mornings women from the village did the laundry at the Rectory and the household washing. This caused great excitement as it was the one link the maids had with the outside world.

Smaller Families

Given the concern with money and given also the increasing education of women in the late nineteenth century it is not surprising that middle-class families tended to get smaller. There was in the nineteenth century some

reaction against the bearing of an excessive number of children. Jane Austen wrote of one woman: 'poor Animal she will be quite worn out before she is 30 . . . I am quite tired of so many children'. Whereas a century or so earlier it might have been necessary to bear ten children to have a family of six, improved diet and medical conditions decreased child mortality dramatically as the nineteenth century progressed. Some limitations on child bearing began to seem desirable.

Birth Control
Generally the Victorians took the attitude that 'the Lord will provide' in maintaining large families, but by 1860 propaganda in favour of birth control began to affect attitudes. An article entitled *The Morality of Married Life* written in 1872 was directed primarily at the middle-class family and recommended the use of the safe-period method of birth control. Books and articles on the subject outraged the respectable Christian Victorian public so much that in 1877 Charles Bradlaugh and Annie Besant were tried for publishing a book called *The Fruits of Philosophy* advocating birth control. They were accused of corrupting 'the subjects of the Queen' and it was stated that they had tried to 'incite and encourage the said subjects to indecent, obscene, unnatural and immoral practices, and bring them to a state of wickedness,

39 *left* A Victorian maid, an essential part of the middle and upper-class household.

40 The nursery staff of a well-to-do home with two nannies and two maids. Only the richer middle-class homes could afford servants on this scale.

lewdness and debauchery. . .'. The whole subject is so clouded in secrecy that it is difficult to know exactly what forms of birth control were advocated.

But however outraged the Victorian public was by birth control propaganda, there is strong evidence that by the end of the nineteenth century the middle classes were beginning to limit their families. By the 1870s it was a commonly-accepted opinion that 'people should not bring into the world any more children than they can reasonably hope to equip in some measure for the fight'.

The desirable number of children in 1850 was considered to be four, but by the end of the century three or even two were considered the norm. This was due on one hand to the economic depression from 1870 to 1900, which though it did not cut the living standards of the middle class, increased those of the lower income groups which made the middle class *seem* poorer. Moreover there was greater concern for education as the century progressed, while school fees were becoming more expensive. The status of the family in the next generation was dependent on good education, as fathers readily admitted:

> We confess to desiring for them [their children] the very best in education that may fit them for stations in life — the higher Civil Service, the Professions, the Navy forsooth: yes even the Church.

Moreover, despite the growth of state education, middle-class families felt that private education was essential, since 'the London Board schools with all their excellent advantages and chances do not appear to offer quite the kind and quality of education that we deem necessary to give our children a fair send off'.

Conclusion

It is difficult to summarize the main changes which took place in family life among the wealthier classes a century or more after the Industrial Revolution. Outstandingly, of course, there was the rise of the distinctive middle-class family. Since the middle classes depended on money made from industry rather than inherited land, financial matters were uppermost in family life; for example the limitation in the size of the family in the late nineteenth century was essentially an economic consideration. Economic factors contributed to the submissiveness of Victorian wives, but later in the century women were achieving greater freedom. But the most important contribution was the idea of home as a place of refuge from the world outside. The aristocratic household was never a refuge; indeed, as the centre of the estate, it was the centre of business. The working-class home was sometimes too squalid to be a refuge — indeed the pub was often a means of escaping from the home. The idea of 'Home Sweet Home' was the Victorian legacy to the modern family.

5
Into the Twentieth Century

The Eden Family

As Britain entered the twentieth century there were powerful agents of economic and social change at work. But on the surface Victorian prosperity and the existing social structure seemed secure. Family life for the landed classes had changed little since the Industrial Revolution, as we can see from Mr Anthony Eden's description of his childhood. The family lived at Windlestone, a substantial nineteenth-century country house in Durham. The family was not large by previous standards, five sons and a daughter, but already above the average certainly for the middle classes by the early twentieth century. A major concern for the family, as always, was the question of inheritance and provision for the younger children. Windlestone and the estate were naturally reserved for the eldest son and Mr Eden's father bought paintings to provide for his younger children. This practice, considered foolish at the time by his gentry neighbours, proved to be extremely wise.

In his book *Another World* Mr Anthony Eden does not give us the number of people in the household, but it was probably substantial. As he says at one point 'faithful retainers are essential ingredients to any understanding of Windlestone before the First World War'. It was a family life in which servants played a crucial role. There was always an agent to oversee the estate, one of whom absconded to the United States with all the cash he could lay his hands on from the Eden house! Then there was Mr Smitton who was Head Keeper, and who 'would without difficulty awe a bold poacher or a restless guest'. Mr Smitton obviously was much concerned with teaching the boys of the family the arts of hunting and shooting. He was evidently a stern master. 'We boys were in considerable awe of Smitton whose rules were strict and whose praise was sparing.' Even on holiday, life was spent amidst servants. Mr Eden was looked after by 'Nannie Ward' while on a family trip to Europe and he was taught by a succession of French and German governesses while the family toured Europe. In addition to the household at Windlestone Mr Eden's father had a flat in London which was looked after by a housekeeper, a cook and a parlourmaid.

Mr Eden's father appears to have had few personal relationships with his children. 'I cannot remember my father ever being present for our Christmas holidays still less taking an active part in arrangements for our games and reading.'

As in the past, the father's role within the family was primarily managerial; he organized the finances and pursued interests which befitted the status of the family.

My father took a dominant and knowledgeable part in the management of a large estate; he was a pioneer in garden design, a good shot, a first class man to hounds and a keen coaching whip, that is to say a skilful conductor of the four in hand. . .

The task of organizing the children's lives fell upon the mother.

Virtually every aspect of our health and upbringing was naturally in our mother's care. My father paid the bills, but my mother did the work, whether in correspondence or by ordering our clothes, packing our trunks for school or visiting us at middle or end of term.

Social Unease in the Upper-Class Family

But strains were already showing in the British economy and British society before the First World War which were to affect upper and middle-class families profoundly. The *Times*, predicting British economic decline, bemoaned the fact that:

others have learned our lessons and bettered our instructions, while we have been too easily contented to rely upon the methods which were effective a generation ago.

H.G. Wells wrote in 1908 that 'all the organizing ideas have slackened, the old habitual bonds have relaxed or altogether become undone'. It is significant that a letter written to the Eden family before 1914 reflects an awareness of the impending decline of the gentry family life style:

The parlourmaid has just walked out of the house without telling anyone she was going and after borrowing a couple of pounds from me. The cook was very angry and to escape from her I dined at a restaurant in Sloane Square close by. My house upon the hill top in Ireland will become a ruin and many houses in England will too; another 50 years will see the end of life as we know it.

41 Mrs Pankhurst, one of the leaders of the suffragette movement, arrested in May 1914 after an attack on Buckingham Palace.

Changes in the Middle Classes

While the upper-class families were to be influenced most profoundly by changing economic conditions, the middle-class family was being subjected to social pressures which were beginning to change the family from within. The Evangelical religious movement which had done much to enhance the ideal of the Victorian family was on the decline. Family religious observance was weakening, family pews were emptying, family prayers were going out of fashion and the family Bible was no longer prominent. But the most powerful factor changing the middle-class family was the extension of women's rights and the assertion by women of a greater degree of independence. Some women at least refused to see themselves existing merely to serve the family. The suffragette Christabel Pankhurst went so far as to write against marriage in 1913:

> For severely practical, common-sensible, sanitary reasons, women are chary of marriage. When the best informed and most experienced medical men say that the majority of men expose themselves before marriage to sexual disease and that only an 'insignificant minority' as one authority puts it — 25 per cent at most — escape infection; when these medical authorities further say that sexual disease is difficult if not impossible to cure, healthy women naturally hesitate to marry.

This was in her book *The Great Scourge and How to End It*. Pankhurst's solution was simple: 'the only cure is votes for women', though one modern author has remarked that antibiotics are more effective! What publications such as Ms Pankhurst's reveal is how far a departure had taken place from

the mid-Victorian concept of the family. There is evidence that some middle-class couples were moving towards new standards as the old ways were attacked. The double standard whereby men could indulge in premarital sex and women not, was questioned. Perhaps one of the best indications of the changes in the family was the insistence of the Royal Commission on Divorce in 1909 which insisted that there is 'no satisfactory solution of the problem raised as to the personal relations between husband and wife. . . except by placing them on an equal footing'.

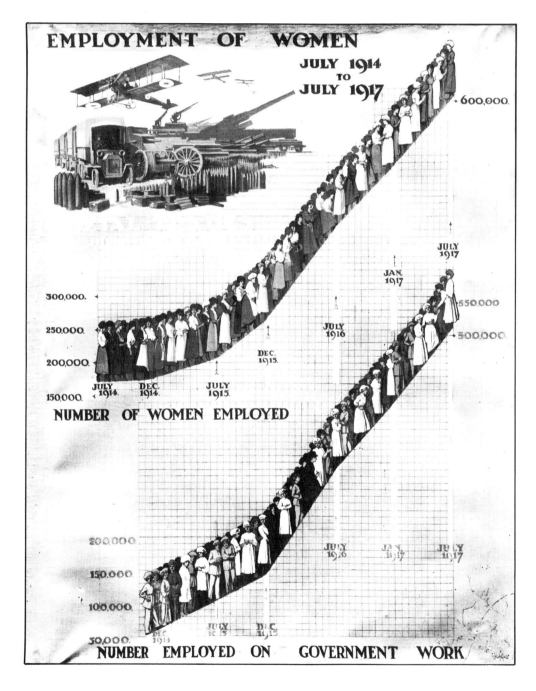

Few of these pressures affected working-class families, the majority of whom were beginning to enjoy a higher standard of living than in the mid-nineteenth century. But if the working-class family was at last beginning to enjoy some of the fruits of the Industrial Revolution, social reformers were able to show that a significant number of families still lived in poverty and suffered from poor health. For example, in 1902 Sir Frederick Maurice stated that 60 per cent of the male population was unfit for military service. Rowntree, in *Poverty, A Study of Town Life,* published in 1901, concluded that 25-30 per cent of the urban population of the UK lived in poverty which he defined as lack of the income necessary to sustain life at an efficient level. This and other surveys showed that low wages rather than idleness were the main cause of poverty. Despite such reports relatively little social legislation was passed before 1914 to help poor families. The 1902 Education Act ensured that working-class children would have a form of secondary education. In 1908 an Old Age Pensions Act was passed providing a pension of up to 5s (25p) a week. This may have enabled a few families to look after ageing parents rather than allowing them to go to the workhouse. In 1911 a Health Act allowed poor wage earners to join the panel of any doctor enrolled in the scheme. These reforms hardly add up to the beginnings of the Welfare State as some historians have suggested, but they do mark the beginnings of State help for the family and the involvement of the State in areas such as education, health and the problems of old age, which previously had been left entirely to the family.

The First World War

It is impossible to assess the effect of the First World War on the family and family life. Its effects were diverse, differing from family to family and class to class. But the most obvious and appalling factor was the loss of men — about three-quarters of a million killed from the British Isles alone, with a further two million wounded. The vast majority were aged between 18 and 35. One of the consequences of this mass killing was that women constituted a slightly higher percentage of the population after 1918.

The emotional impact of the war on families must have been great, but difficult to document. Anthony Eden in his memoirs points out the agony of the married man returning to the front:

> whatever we youngsters may have felt about returning to battle we had no claim to sympathy compared with the married officer. For him and his wife it really did hurt, with an added haunting fear if they had young children and the soldier, sailor or airman, were the breadwinner. Theirs was a true courage.

42   A graph showing the spectacular rise in the number of women employed from July 1914 to July 1917.

43 A woman working in a munitions factory at Vickers in July 1915, doing a job which would normally have been done by a man.

It is even more difficult to trace the emotional impact of the returning troops. Sometimes wounded, they and their families had to adjust again to civilian family life after years of upheaval.

Certain changes affecting the family clearly emerged from the war. The trend towards greater freedom for women was accelerated. Not only did the war offer a wide variety of jobs to women which had previously been barred to them, but women received great public recognition for their war efforts.

Munitions Minister E.S. Montague declared that 'our armies have been saved and victory assured by the women in the munitions factories'. Women's courage was widely noted such as in the report of Dr Elsie Inglis and the Scottish Women's Hospitals working in Serbia:

It is extraordinary how these women endure hardships; they refuse help, and carry the wounded themselves. They work like navvies. No wonder England is a great country if the women are like that.

(A. Marwick, *The Deluge*)

Changing Moral Standards

The First World War also resulted in an undermining of the Victorian ideal of female chastity. There were a number of reasons for this, including a decline in religious fervour.

The religious teaching that the body was the temple of the Holy Ghost could mean little or nothing to those who saw it mutilated and destroyed in millions by Christian nations engaged in war. All moral standards were held for a short time and irretrievably lost. Little wonder that the old ideas of chastity and self control in sex were, for many, also lost.

During the war many women left home to live in hostels or lodgings; also, the decline of the chaperone in upper-class families contributed to greater sexual freedom for women.

44 Women's Land Army marching through London in October 1918. A quarter of a million women worked on the land in the First World War, replacing the male labourers who were away fighting.

Chaperones were to disappear for ever, and during the war they were hard at work 'canteening' and so on, and people who gave parties didn't want to feed and water them. And if they were elderly they didn't feel like having to walk home after late nights.

The increased use of contraceptives during and after the war contributed to greater sexual freedom and a reduction in the average size of families, though it did not prevent a considerable number of illegitimate 'war babies' in 1915 and after. Troops were given contraceptives during the war and their use spread in Britain. 'When I left England in 1911', commented Sir Bruce Lockhart, 'contraceptives were hard to buy outside London or other large cities. By 1919 every village chemist was selling them.'

However, despite the upheavals described, the effects of war on the family can be exaggerated. The changing status of women, changing moral standards and the use of contraceptives largely affected middle-class women and middle-class families. The working-class woman already had the opportunity for working outside the house, and her moral attitudes were much more dictated by the community in which she lived than by current female literature. It would appear that the use of contraception spread only slowly among working-class families. Moreover, the effects of war might have destroyed the Victorian middle-class family, but there is no evidence that the middle-class family did not successfully adjust to changed circumstances. Though divorce figures increased after the war, so did the number of divorcees who remarried. The

45 A chirpy clippie! Yet another job which women began to do in World War I.

destruction of the Victorian family code began the development which we have today, when, according to one writer, there is a 'growing capacity and willingness to ground familial relationships in the practice of social and personal equality, and to substitute knowledge for ignorance as the basis of conduct'.

Delinquency

If the emancipation of women had little effect on working-class families, the greater freedom for young men resulting from the war affected all families, but possibly the working class family more than any other. The growing problem of junevile delinquency was already a source of concern during the war. The National Council of Public Morals found a ready scapegoat in the cinema:

> It is strongly alleged and widely believed that the picture house is responsible for the increase in juvenile crime and that boys are often led to imitate crimes (larceny and burglary) which they have seen in the pictures.
>
> (A. Marwick, *The Deluge*)

A report of the Departmental Committee on Juvenile Education of 1917 was much more perceptive and saw the causes in social factors connected with the war:

> Parental control, so far as it formerly existed, has been relaxed, largely through the absence of families from their homes. Wages have been exceptionally high, and although this has led to an improved standard of living, it has also in ill-regulated households induced habits of foolish and mischievous extravagance. . . Gambling has increased. Excessive hours of strenuous labour have overtaxed the powers of young people; while many have taken advantage of the extraordinary demand for juvenile labour to change even more rapidly than usual from one blind alley employment to another.
>
> (A. Marwick, *The Deluge*)

The mourning for the youth lost in the war developed into an adulation of the young. The young were more in touch with the new forces of the twenties and they became social trendsetters. This was partly based on a solid economic consequence of the war, when there was a revolution in the sex and age-earning pattern in Britain and young people and women were earning a higher proportion of total wages than ever before. The inter-war years marked the beginning of a trend leading to the affluent teenager of the 1960s. Relationships in the family were naturally affected by these developments. The iron authoritarianism of the Victorian father was gradually modified. But the full effects of these changes were not seen until after the Second World War, and between the wars the authority structure of the family remained in fact remarkably sound considering the pressures upon it.

Inter-War Years

There were contradictory economic and social forces operating on families in the inter-war years. Particularly in the depression of the 1930s, a number of the lower aristocratic and old middle-class families lost their wealth and position. Many town houses around what had been exclusive London squares were sold and converted into flats. New suburban residential areas such as Putney were developed, where no one of any social note had lived before. As servants became increasingly difficult to get and expensive to keep, serious consideration was given to labour-saving devices in the home and also to

46 At the turn of the century there were still numerous examples of slums such as these in Glasgow, even though working-class conditions were improving.

47 Houses in Stepney, East London, about 1909. The houses look substantial but probably lacked light and air. The closeness of the houses produced closely knit families and communities which characterize the East End of London even today.

smaller houses. These suburbs were particularly the preserve of an emerging new middle class, a middle class who ran industry and the professions, unlike the old middle class who *owned* industry.

By and large working-class families continued to increase their standard of living, which we have noted began to rise in the late nineteenth century. The gradual decrease of family size contributed significantly to this. Moreover between 1914 and 1937 average working hours were reduced slightly, while the average earnings of employed workers nearly doubled. Council houses, though monotonous in design, were of a fairly high minimum standard of size, lighting and ventilation. Council house building made a major contribution to lifting the standard of housing of the mass of the population, and though it was a sign of being working class to live in a council house, the comforts were considerable. As a recent historian put it:

> a council house carried with it the implication of lower-class status, but the difference between the new council houses and the cheaper middle-class homes was minimal, and in reality the gap in living conditions which divided the lower middle class from the council house tenants was very narrow and in some cases non-existent.

Unemployment

The atmosphere of growing expectations made the unemployment of the thirties more difficult to bear, and inevitably put great strain on the family. A village carpenter spoke of the tensions arising from both himself and his sons being on the dole. Speaking of his wife he said:

> her one complaint other than the money seems to be the congestion of the cottage. When all are at home the whole day long, as sometimes happens, we fill up every available bit of space and get in each other's way, and on each other's nerves. For I have got three sons and two of them are nearly as much as I am. Our cottage is very small for four adults.

The most important effect of the thirties' unemployment on the family, however, seems to have been the loss of self respect and thereby authority of the father. Where father was on the dole, mother often became the wage earner and father was forced into what sociologists call 'role reversal', or more simply they exchanged jobs. A man who had been a wire drawer in an iron and steel works until he was made redundant, described his life:

> I do the housework after my wife has left home to go to work at half-past seven in the morning. I read, I play with the child, I go for walks in the evening after my wife has returned. Is this a man's life?

48 A nineteenth-century painting which suggests the worry and despair of a family when father was out of work.

Being the breadwinner was so important to most men that failure in this respect brought deep personal shame and embarrassment to the whole family. The same wire drawer said:

> Any long spell of unemployment leaves you with little to be proud of and much to be ashamed of. Our child is still too young to realize that it is her mother who works. We carefully keep her from knowing it. She is not likely to learn what it implies from her playmates, for there is little to choose in the circumstances of most working families in this town.

A London housepainter who had been on the dole for a number of years believed that his authority in the family had been totally undermined:

> Family life is made more difficult and, unfortunately, those difficulties tend to become permanent and to my mind are one of the worst results of unemployment. My wife, not at first realizing the difficulty of obtaining employment, used often to make unnecessary remarks implying I not only did not seek work, but was lazy. These remarks with both our tempers rattled naturally led to quarrels. These quarrels were overheard and impressed themselves on the minds of our children. The idea seemed to be entered in their minds that mother's view was correct, with the consequent result that they are less apt to consider one worthy of their love, or a fitting person to ask if they require advice or direction. . .

The diets of families on the dole tended to be deficient, as one might expect. Reports in the 1930s commented on the lack of fresh fruit, vegetables and salads. Most were below what the Ministry of Health considered to be the minimum calorie content, but by far the most serious deficiency was a poor supply of milk. It is interesting that a report in December 1976, *I Dread to Think about Christmas* by Shiela Cliff and Frank Field, stated that poor families still tended not to buy 'butter, fresh meat, fresh fruit and vegetables'.

The 'Traditional Working-Class Family'

In addition to the pressures imposed by the First World War, certain longer-term factors were producing what some sociologists like to term the 'traditional working-class family'. This family was the product of the Industrial Revolution and the improved living standards of the late nineteenth and early twentieth century.

One of the most outstanding features of the 'traditional working-class family' is the importance of the mother. It is the mother who has the close links with the children, and it is mother who tends to keep the family together by visiting and inviting back relatives. The close ties between mother and child are of course biological, but the remoteness of the child from the father was certainly increased by industrialization when the father was out of the home so much. This has always been a feature of upper-class households, but not of the working classes. The close ties between the mother and her children and in particular between the mother and her daughter, have been illustrated by several sociological studies.

In his book *The People of Ship Street*, for example, Kerr gives numerous examples of this relationship. A married woman of 39 with five children commented: 'I couldn't get on without me mother. I could get on without me husband. I don't notice him'.

Within the nuclear family the mother may always have been considered the protector of children from the authoritarianism of the father. Only if mother choosed to punish did the children really get worried. 'When father beats us we hide behind our Mum; when me Mother beats us I run out on the street'. The feeling of the importance and power of mother was often instilled into children at an early age. A child of 13 said: 'Me Mother says "you can get another father but you won't get another mother" and that's true isn't it?'. Ruth went on to say that should her mother die and her father remarry she would run away from home and persuade her brothers and sisters to do likewise.

The close dependence on the womenfolk in the family partly results no doubt from the fact that in an industrial society men have such an independent life outside the family structure. J. Klein in his *Sample from English Culture* examines this pattern in a mining community in Ashton. The separation from the home starts with adolescence when a youth starts work. The youths in Ashton spent most of their leisure time in groups of half a dozen males, going to football, playing billiards or drinking. When a young man begins 'courting strong' the group reacts with strongly discouraging noises, 'Wee we'd ask thee to come for a pint but we expect tha's off to get they feet under t' table.' — that is, he's settling down with one woman. The young man will probably play down his emotional ties with the girl because this is 'unmanly' and justify the time spent with her by obliquely suggesting that she allows him sexual intercourse. Klein comments that in the group's behaviour we see the beginning of what will be a continual conflict between home and other ties.

Conflict within the home appeared to be part of family life in Ashton. Disagreement between husband and wife was essentially concerned with the question 'in which sector of the community shall the money be spent — in the family or at the pub or club?'. One 18-year old, newly married, explained that quarrelling was something of a ritual. 'We have a row regularly every Saturday when I ask him for my wage and he doesn't want to take me out with him'. Both Kerr and Klein in their respective studies concluded that husband and wife tend to lead separate lives and have little to talk about. Marriages were a matter of 'carry on pure and simple'. So long as the man works and gave his wife and family sufficient money and the woman used her family 'wage' wisely and gave her husband the few things he demands, the marriage would carry on!

Though the studies of both Klein and Kerr were made after the Second World War, the family life they analyze was very much formed in the earlier part of the twentieth century. It is true that men have always sought pubs as a refuge from home, but it was the Industrial Revolution which produced such tightly-knit male communities, from which women are excluded. In farming communities, for example, husbands and wives at least have their work in common, as the wife inevitably worked on the farm. Moreover with the improved economic standards of the twenties and thirties, men could spend money at the pub without ruining their families. Amid nineteenth-century poverty, the drinking man was a destroyer of the family, but in the twentieth century drinking and family obligations are not contradictory — though they do lead to tensions.

Extended Family and Kinship

When we talk of the 'extended family' we mean a household which includes relatives other than mother, father and children, such as grandparents, sons and daughters-in-law or even uncles and aunts. Households comprising just parents and children are known as nuclear families, and it has often been argued that the decline from the extended and supportive family to the isolated nuclear family is one of the main causes of our family problems. But except for the upper classes it seems highly unlikely that many people were ever part of an extended family. Peter Laslett, in his various population studies, has argued convincingly that in England the nuclear family was the normal arrangement and recently Michael Anderson in his studies of industrial Lancashire has offered good reasons why the extended family emerged — albeit briefly — at the end of the nineteenth and the beginning of the twentieth century.

Anderson found that in the textile towns the practice of grandparents living with the family was widespread by the mid-nineteenth century. He attributed this to the fact that old relatives could in fact substantially increase the family income by caring for the children while the mother of the home worked in the factory. Later the practice spread to other parts of the country because of changing social and economic conditions. As poverty declined in the twentieth century, so the disadvantages of taking in a dependent relative were not so great. Moreover the smaller size of the average family meant that there was more space for 'Gran'. Large working-class families fitted into their homes in earlier times only because everyone left home as soon as possible! On the other hand with a shortage of housing between the wars it became common practice for daughters to bring their husbands to live with 'Mum' for the first few years of marriage.

A similar pattern can be seen in the extent to which the family keeps up close contact with and helps its relatives outside the household. Sociologists call this relationship 'kinship'. Many modern critics of the family have pointed to the decline of kinship as another sign of the deterioration of the traditional family. But it is doubtful if there was a great deal of kinship of among working-class families in the nineteenth century. Comments from mid-nineteenth century Preston suggest that most families were too poor to give assistance to their relatives and if the relatives lived a few miles away contact was not maintained except for the family rituals of births, marriages and deaths. But twentieth-century conditions have been more favourable to maintaining close family ties. As communities became more settled after the upheaval of industrialization, and as transport improved dramatically, contact between relatives was greater. But above all as families became better off they were able to help poorer relatives, and in particular aged parents. Moreover social legislation such as the 1908 Pension Act for the old enabled families to give assistance without endangering their own economic security. This contrasts with what Anderson found in nineteenth-century Lancashire when the possibility of assistance to relatives was severely limited by the costs which it incurred, unless such kin could either bring in some income through employment or the Poor Law authorities were prepared to help.

Conclusions

It is difficult to summarize the bewildering variety of changes which influenced the family before the Second World War. The inter-war years saw the eclipse of the aristocratic household, while middle-class women tended to be less subordinate to their husbands than in the nineteenth century. All families were beginning to feel the challenge from a youth that was less easily subdued, but serious threats to the family structure never emerged. Amongst working-class families many of the features we associate with the traditional family were formed in the aftermath of industrialization — the strict separation of functions between husband and wife and the power of mother in the home. There were probably a greater number of extended families and more kinship relations. But for all these changes one fact stands out clearly: the family continued to be the main unit of society and adapted to the profound changes of the twentieth century possibly with increased strength. The family was strong enough at any rate to withstand another world war.

49   The radio brought a new focus to home life between the two wars. Here we see a family clustered round the new invention.

6
The Modern Family

There can have been few times in history when the family as an institution has received such attention as it does today. Many writers believe that the family is in decline. Such critics agree that the nuclear family is too isolated because it lacks the support of grandparents and relatives. Also it is argued that the Welfare State, developed since 1945, has taken over so many of the functions of the family that the family is now a mere shadow of its former self. Bertrand Russell made this point about the State's power in his book *Marriage and Morals*:

> So, far from having power of life and death over his children as the Roman father had, the British father is liable to be prosecuted for cruelty if he treats his child as most fathers 100 years ago would have thought essential for a moral upbringing. The State provides medical and dental care and feeds the child if the parents are destitute. The functions of the father are reduced to a minimum since most of them have been taken over by the State.

He goes on to conclude that, as a result of this, the family is declining.

> Although the law means to uphold the family it has in modern times increasingly intervened between parents and children and is gradually becoming, against the wishes and intentions of law-makers, one of the chief engines for the break-up of the family system.

As we know, children can now in fact be taken away from their parents and placed under the care of a local authority if a court decides that the parents are unfit to look after their own children. Along the same lines, Bryan Wilson, in an article on the teacher's role, wrote that the family had been reduced to a

> highly specialized agency for affection. It has lost the other types of social activity which were once so much a part of its activities -- the work-place, the dance hall, the youth club and other institutions have taken over its economic and recreational functions, and its political and religious functions were lost long ago.

Certain points in the above statements are beyond dispute. The State has increasingly intervened in many aspects of family life and individuals now spend more time outside the home than in previous centuries. But both these developments could well strengthen the family rather than damage it. When the home was both the work place and the only centre of recreation the tensions within the family might have been greater than today and there is plenty of evidence of violence within the family in the past. Moreover the State has generally intervened to improve and help families improve standards — standards of care, health and housing. Bearing in mind such developments, Ronald Fletcher in his book *The Family and Marriage in Britain* has concluded that the modern family is in good health.

Marriage and the Family have not declined in our time, but have improved in most respects. If we have problems — and we have of course many, they are to be properly understood in terms of complex changes and deliberately

50   Lord Beveridge: The Beveridge Report of 1942 formed the basis of social legislation on which the Welfare State was developed after the Second World War.

attempted improvements (of the social, legal, political and economic kinds) rather than in terms of some kind of moral deterioration of the family as such . . . I do not know of any other period of British history in which the qualities and expectation of marriage and parenthood — in personal, social or legal terms — were of as high a standard (and for the *whole* population) as they are now.

Second World War

We shall examine the validity of the opinions expressed above, but first we must look at the formative influences on the family since 1945. Certainly the most dramatic, and for some traumatic, was the impact of the Second World War. For some families disruption began two days before the declaration of war, for on September 1st 1939 the Government began to move about a million and a half people from the crowded cities of Britain. The majority of these were mothers and children, transferred with teachers and escorts to safer areas in the countryside. Some 50 per cent of all schoolchildren left towns such as Manchester and London while some 35 per cent of mothers and young children also left the capital.

Evacuation

The effect of evacuation on families in the long term is difficult to assess, but in the short term it was often traumatic. As the official historian on social problems in the war, Professor Titmuss, wrote:

> To be torn up from the roots of home life and to be sent away from the family circle, in most instances for the first time in the child's life, was a painful event. The whole of the child's life and all the deep emotional ties that bound it to its parents, were suddenly disrupted. From the first day of September 1939 evacuation ceased to be a problem of administrative planning. It became instead a multitude of problems in human relationships.

The difficulties of evacuation presented themselves immediately when the children, some with their mothers, some without, arrived at their destination point. There was no pre-arranged plan to place them in particular houses. Country families who had agreed to take in evacuees turned up at the railway station or village hall and 'scenes reminiscent of a cross between an early Roman slave market and Selfridge's bargain basement ensued'. Moreover some groups found it difficult to get a home in the reception area:

> The hardest group of all to billet were the mothers with several children. Such difficulties often occurred among Roman Catholic parties from Liverpool and Glasgow for the mother refused to be parted from her children. . . Not infrequently they took the next train home.

51 An evacuated family enjoying the security of the countryside in 1939. Not all evacuees, however, found their surroundings to their liking.

52 The evacuation of London school children: a soldier on leave says goodbye to his young son pathetically clutching a parcel of possessions.

One of the first consequences of emotional stress amongst evacuated children was an increase in incontinence. In most cases this cleared up as the children got to know their foster parents and became used to the country, but bed wetting remained a problem for a small percentage of evacuated children and naturally this was highlighted by the press. 'No other aspect of the social results of evacuation received so much publicity or lent itself so easily to exaggeration and misunderstanding'.

Evacuation made people more aware of existing family problems. Despite the increased living standards experienced by many between the wars, a number of city children were badly clothed, a fact which appalled some of their foster parents. A typical report to the Ministry of Health complained that:

> many Manchester and Liverpool little girls have never worn knickers, a fact which distresses and horrifies the foster parents. A large percentage have never possessed sleeping units, but take off the outer clothing and sleep in their underwear (the latter frequently being father's old shirt pinned and/or stitched to fit its new purpose). Few have ever possesssed a best outfit.

Wartime Housing Problems

The war intensified other existing problems. In large cities such as London, Birmingham, Glasgow and Hull the housing problems grew worse when no homes were built and war damage was not made good. By the end of 1942, according to official estimates, one million people in England and Wales were living in houses which, but for the war, would have been condemned as slums. By 1943 there had been a great decrease in school attendance due to war disruption. Schools were in a very poor condition. 'The education system as a whole did not collapse, but in a number of areas it came near to doing so.' An even more acute problem was that many families found themselves without fathers. By 1943 some 30 per cent of all British men were in the armed forces, Civil Defence and other services. Moreover mothers also were frequently out of the home — some 55 per cent of women between 18 and 40 years of age were in the services or industry. 'This great withdrawal from the home was not good for children. It meant less order and less stability.'

Social Effects of War

The problems created by the Second World War for families prompted some critics to see family life as crumbling. In a letter to the *Times* in February 1947, Mr D.R. Mae of Marriage Guidance wrote that 'the family life of our time stands indicted', and the Archbishop of Westminster complained that 'morality has declined. I need only point to the ever increasing number of divorces, murders, suicides and robberies'; and he held declining family life responsible. But what is far more striking about families in the war is how they kept together despite all the difficulties and problems. There were only a few evacuated children deserted by their parents. Professor Titmuss concluded that:

> viewed against the background of the immense social upheavals of six years of war, these residual problems of parental care were, in terms of numbers, insignificant.

What is also significant is the fact that after the initial agreement to evacuation, many parents brought back their children to live with them in the city so that the family could keep together. Indeed the strength of the family unit was an important factor in helping people face the hazards of war.

53 *opposite left*   Londoners sleeping in an air-raid shelter during the Second World War. The disruption of ordinary family life was obviously great and the absence of children reminds us how many had been evacuated.

54 *opposite right*   As with the First World War, there was a great increase in the number of women working in factories after 1939, especially producing armaments. This photograph is entitled 'making beautiful bombs'.

55 *right*   During the Second World War housing conditions worsened and despite the post-war programme for slum clearance appalling conditions such as this one-roomed flat in the Gorbals area of Glasgow remained.

56 By the 1950s slum clearance was under way, but often to be replaced by high-rise flats, as seen above. Recently high-rise flats have been largely blamed for producing a wide range of social problems.

The social problems created by the Second World War were similar to those created by the First World War. The increase in juvenile delinquency was marked and began to receive great attention in the media. But the desire to improve social conditions which had also been present in 1918 was translated into practice after 1945. In that year William Beveridge introduced the provisions of the Welfare State which extended old-age pensions and insurance schemes and provided a free health service for the whole family. In 1944 a new Education Act had been introduced which made secondary education compulsory for all children and raised the school leaving age from 14 to 15.

Post-War Years
Economic conditions in the late 1940s were rather grim — utility clothing was too thin for real comfort, while eggs, meat and coal were in short supply. Nevertheless the post-war period, especially the 1950s, saw a real improvement in living standards for the mass of the people. Rowntree's study of York in 1951 showed that the proportion of working-class people living below the poverty line (which had been revised upwards in response to changing contemporary standards) had fallen from 31 per cent in 1936 to 3 per cent in 1950. The welfare service was mainly responsible for this improvement, for without it Rowntree estimated that some 22 per cent of working-class families would still be below poverty level. When Mr Harold Macmillan, the then Prime Minister, announced to the nation in the late fifties that 'you've never had it so good', he expressed the feelings that many families were indeed experiencing. This new prosperity continued into the sixties when Britain acquired a public image as the 'swinging' centre of Europe in fashion and pop music. Rising living standards were checked from the late sixties when the British economy began to experience difficulties, while in the mid-seventies many families have suffered a fall in standards. Nevertheless, vast improve-

ments since 1945 are beyond doubt. Consequently:

> the vast majority of families do not have to cope with the abrasive effects of chronic poverty. Arguments about the choice of T.V. programmes are better than traumatic arguments over arrangements for sharing a single bed, the distribution of meagre food allowances, or rent money for some miserable hovel.

The Post-War Family

The post-war period has also seen changes in the size of, and personal relationships within, the family. Ronald Fletcher in his book *The Family and Marriage in Britain* lists the main characteristics of today's family. The family is started earlier than in previous times and therefore is likely to be of longer duration. The British family is likely to be consciously planned; consequently it is likely to be small in size. The norm is the nuclear family — that is mother, father and children only, living in the house. Grandparents and relatives will tend to live in separate households. Moreover the family will be based on a marriage that, hopefully, 'has been entered into and maintained on a completely voluntary basis by partners of equal status'. The modern family tends to show more concern for the care and upbringing of children than in previous times and is sometimes called 'child-centred'. Moreover the importance of the family is recognized by the Government, which provides a wide range of educational and social services to aid the family.

One of the most significant changes in the post-war family has been in the position of women, resulting in a changed relationship between husband and wife. Middle-class women began to achieve greater independence after the

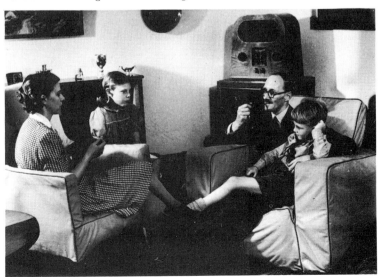

57 Sir Harold Macmillan as Prime Minister in 1955. He led Britain from the years of post-war austerity to a decade of relative affluence.

58 This photograph, taken in 1947, shows the post-war ideal of father, mother and two children listening to the radio together.

First World War, but the traditional working-class family in which there was a complete separation of roles — mother in the kitchen and father in the pub! — continued between the wars. Doubtless the situation still exists, but Young and Willmott in their study of Bethnal Green in the East End of London, found that younger working-class families differed greatly from the older generation (see Ronald Fletcher, *The Family and Marriage in Britain):*

> The younger husband of today does not consider that the children belong exclusively to the wife's world or that he can abandon them to her (and her mother) while he takes his comfort in the male atmosphere of the pub. He now shares the responsibility for the number of children as well as for their welfare after they are born.

This change has been so profound that Young and Willmott concluded that:

> impressions suggest that the old style of working-class family is fast disappearing. The husband portrayed by the previous social investigators is no longer true to life. In place of the old comes a new kind of companionship between man and woman, reflecting the rise in status of the young wife and children which is one of the great transformations of our time. . .

When we contrast this with the findings of the sociologists quoted in the last chapter on traditional working-class marriage, we can see a fundamental social change at work.

Attitudes to Children

Children, too, are today being treated differently inside the family. Whereas nineteenth-century fathers ruled the household with a rod of iron, today's children are less likely to be beaten for disobedience. Some critics believe that the lack of harsh discipline is a loss. We are, they say, producing children who are too self centred, and who are consequently less prepared than previous generations to meet their duties to society. It is enormously difficult to judge the validity of such accusations. Certainly children are less prepared to accept the edicts of their parents or society without question. On the other hand the enormous amount of charitable work done by young people also shows concern for the elderly, the poor and less advantaged members of society. Moreover we can say with confidence that in the small modern family children have never before had such opportunities for enjoying physical and mental health and for developing their talents to the full. Parents are more concerned than they used to be to see their children develop fully. Mr. Gordon Bessey, an education officer, commented at a conference on The Family that 'all concerned with the education of children outside the home are more conscious than ever before of the deep interest of an increasing number of parents in their children's welfare and their education'. The relaxation of discipline in the family is in keeping with the more personal relationships between man and wife and a reflection of the greater care and attention that can be given to children in the small family.

Working Wives

An increasing number of women now go out to work. Between 1931 and 1951 the number of married women at work trebled and about half of Britain's female work force today is married. Such a trend has caused concern and a few years ago much was written about 'latch-key' children — children who let themselves into the house after school because mother was at work. But whether working mothers lead to child neglect is far from certain: the problem has not yet been fully studied. What studies have been carried out suggest that the woman's motives for going out to work are for the good of the family rather than to escape from family responsibilities. The Social Science Department at the London School of Economics studied the lives of 300 women workers at Peak Freen (the biscuit manufacturers) in Bermondsey. The studies concluded that (see Ronald Fletcher's book):

> mothers made arrangements with, and received the willing help of, their husbands and their own mothers in order to make sure that their children were adequately cared for . . . . There is no evidence here, then, of child neglect on the part of working mothers. On the contrary the picture is one of family concern. Indeed some of these women argued 'that the neglectful mother is not the one who works but the one who is too lazy or indifferent to take advantage of today's opportunities to raise her family's standards'.

Whatever the critics may say about working wives they are surely part of the modern family. Their earnings help to satisfy the desire for an improved standard of living, while at the same time an independent wage provides the woman with status and encourages a more equal partnership between husband and wife. A recent study in the USA, for example, found that working wives were less submissive to their husbands than those who stayed at home. In the long term it is necessary to extend child care (through such facilities as nursery schools which in 1977 were being cut because of Government economies) and rearrange women's hours of work so that there is as little clash as possible between a woman's role as a mother and as a worker.

Divorce

One of the most significant factors within marriage and the family which has changed over the past 50 years is the incidence of divorce. There was a sharp increase in divorce around 1918 and then a fall (but not to pre-war level) until 1939. Divorce figures went up again during the war years, reaching a peak in post-war 1947. Then there were three years of decline until legal aid was introduced in 1950. Although there was some fall in the incidence of divorce in the 1950s, the trend since 1960 has again been towards increasing divorce. The Divorce Reform Act of 1969, along with other legislation such as the Maintenance Orders Act of 1968, has made divorce a more practical proposition for many. The Divorce Act of 1969 recognized 'irretrievable breakdown' as sufficient cause for divorce, so that marriages could be dissolved without accusing the other of wrongdoing, and without the existence of a 'guilty party' in the marriage. But this increase in the divorce rates must be seen in context, as the Registrar General pointed out in 1967.

> With the strong propensity to marriage and falling age at marriage, the recent increase in the number of marriages that fail, measured by the number of divorces absolute, is brought into proper perspective and the task of seeking the cause of the increase is made somewhat less difficult.

One of the factors that does emerge clearly from divorce statistics is that there is a strikingly higher rate of divorce among those marrying in the younger age groups. For example the average duration of marriages dissolved in 1966 was over 13 years, but for those marrying under 20 it was just over 11 years. Moreover the most vulnerable marriages seem to belong to those who marry before the age of 20 because the girl is pregnant. Though increased divorce figures are saddening, they should not be seen as a sign of a less-than-serious attitude to marriage and the family, as Fletcher is at pains to point out:

> This means that the increased resort to divorce which the statistics portray, though no doubt resting on changed attitudes towards the termination of marriage, by no means indicates, in any simple and definite way, any change in the stability of the family, in the desire for such stability, or in the attitudes of responsibility in seeking it.

Functions of the Family

Because of economic and social changes the family does not control all aspects of the life of its members as it did in the past. The family is no longer a unit of production as it was before the Industrial Revolution, nor is the home the centre of education as it was before the full development of our present schools system. The provisions under the National Health service likewise have changed the ways in which the family is responsible for the health of its members.

In many ways however the family remains an important economic unit. Although fewer women now bake their own bread and make all the clothes for the family, the household still needs to be organized. Mother is still generally responsible for buying and cooking the food. Likewise she still has to ensure a plentiful supply of clean clothes in a good state of repair — the Welfare State has not taken over this function!

Advertisers are certainly in no doubt that the modern family is an important economic unit of consumption. Even as early as 1959 Mark Abrams, in a radio talk entitled 'The Home Centred Society', argued that much more money was being spent on household goods since the Second World War:

> The proportion of families with a vacuum cleaner has doubled, ownership of a refrigerator has trebled, owners of a washing machine have increased tenfold; we have stocked our homes with vastly more furniture, radiograms, carpets, space heaters, water heaters and armchairs. . .

The argument that the Welfare State has stripped the family of its economic functions is not convincing. On the contrary recent laws have tried to help and support the family. If families find themselves in financial difficulties because the father is unemployed or lowly paid, the State will provide money such as 'supplementary benefits' to keep the family together, whereas in the nineteenth century the family might have ended in the workhouse. Likewise if divorce occurs, the State attempts to ensure that the wife receives sufficient maintenance money to keep her and the children, if she has custody of them. These legal changes were observed by a recent writer when he said that:

> the law of social security, like the law of maintenance, is more realistic than the law of property; account is being taken in these branches of law of the existence of the household as an economic unit and the natural inequalities in the economic functions of husband and wife.

Education

When we turn to the question of education it is surely clear that the family is still vitally important in providing education for its children, though the nature of this provision has changed. In the years before formal schooling starts, the family is important in 'socializing' the child, in developing its speech and behaviour patterns and in some cases teaching the basic skills such as reading. Moreover with smaller families and a much greater emphasis on child care, this role is likely to be taken much more seriously than it was a century ago.

Once a child starts school the attitude of the parents to education is probably vital in determining the child's subsequent development. It is generally recognized that parents who take a close interest in the value of education are more likely to produce children who succeed at school. Moreover parents can help their children considerably if they are familiar with the different types of schools, colleges and universities and the kinds of jobs which might result from different courses.

Brian Jackson and Dennis Marsden, writing in 1965, considered that many working-class children were at a disadvantage simply because their parents had less knowledge on such subjects than their middle-class counterparts. Working-class parents:

> wanted to know what physics *was,* and what kinds of jobs it opened for a girl; they wanted to know whether you could do anything with a history qualification other than teach more history. They wanted to know the differences between a training college and a university in nature, quality, time and cost.

It seems likely that knowledge of the educational system is greater today, but the onus is still on the family, on parents, to guide their children through the system.

Health

The family's functions in the sphere of health must also be said to have increased rather than diminished. For all the specialization of modern medicine and the extensive health service provided by the State, the family is still central to health. It is the family which is responsible for the diet and environment of its individual members — vital factors in good health. Studies concerning mental health have emphasized the importance of the family. Fletcher, in *The Family and Marriage in Britain*, concludes that:

> with the insistence of modern psychology upon the fact that the earliest years of the child's experience in the family are of supreme importance for the subsequent development of his or her adult personality, it might

59 Child welfare clinics such as this one at Harold Hill Health Centre have done much to improve the care of children and reduce child mortality.

60 Dr Benjamin Spock, the American doctor and author. Spock's writings on child rearing were influential especially among the middle classes, in producing a less authoritarian attitude by parents towards their children.

be said that an almost completely new dimension has been added to the concern for health within the modern family. Parents are now thought to be responsible not only for the physical health of their children, but also for the secure and healthy development of the child's whole personality.

Environmental Effects on Children

The importance of the family in the development of children's personalities and achievements is so great that there is a danger of exaggeration. In 1972, the then Secretary of State for Social Services, Sir Keith Joseph, made a major speech on the question of poverty and deprivation. He argued that poverty breeds poverty and that the same families are deprived, generation after generation. If a child is born into such a deprived family, only positive help or 'discrimination' by the social welfare services can prevent his or her poverty in the next generation. This belief was accepted by a great many people until the publication of a recent book by Michael Rutter and Nicola Madge. *Cycles of Disadvantage* found that there was little evidence to support the idea that poverty continues in the same family from generation to generation. Professor Rutter says that there is some evidence that the wealthy in one generation are frequently related to the wealthy in the next. But for the poor probably the most startling finding is that 'discontinuities in almost all forms of disadvantage are more common than continuities'. Over half of all forms of disadvantage (such as poverty, unemployment or even illness) arise anew each generation. Even in regions where continuity is strongest many individuals break out of the cycle and on the other hand many people become disadvantaged without having been reared by disadvantaged parents.

Even the widespread belief that broken homes tend to produce children whose marriages are more likely to be unstable needs to be seen in perspective. It is true that a recent study has shown that the risk of divorce or separation was more than doubled for individuals whose parents had been divorced or separated, but 75 per cent of divorced or separated individuals in the present generation come from intact homes in the previous generation. Moreover over three-quarters of children from broken homes make successful marriages which remain intact.

Trends for the Future

A number of the characteristics of the modern family are likely to continue in the forseeable future. The improved status of women is here to stay. Despite the economic depression of the mid-1970s, working women have become an essential part of the economy and a significant number in the future will wish to combine a career with the task of bringing up a family. The same is true of the improved status of children. The freer atmosphere and less rigid discipline within the family may have made life more difficult for parents, but it seems highly unlikely that a subsequent generation will impose Victorian rules on their children. Moreover the economic independence of teenagers, able to earn as much as their fathers in some cases, would undermine any attempt at extending formal discipline to this age group.

The tendency towards earlier marriage seems likely to continue. In marriage the relationship of husband and wife will increasingly be based on affection and companionship, quite apart from the having and rearing of children; and we should not forget that this is a twentieth-century innovation, at least for the middle and upper classes. Many couples will have completed the child-rearing period at an early age, given early marriages and small families. Especially after the child-rearing period of their family life, marriage will become a matter of personal companionship.

Certain problems will doubtless recur. Both battered babies and battered wives are subject to serious concern today; in recent years much more care and attention has been given to these problems. The stresses of family life will always expose weak personalities as well as support them; and the strain of dealing with difficult babies will always lead to some harassed mothers — or fathers — maltreating them. But these problems receive the attention they do today because the standards of child care are generally high. In the past, violence was so much the norm that short of murder parents were seldom reprimanded for beating their children.

A problem which could intensify is the isolation of the nuclear family. With the father moving jobs more often, the family of the future is even less likely than today to live near its immediate relatives, though this does not necessarily mean that contact is not maintained with such relatives, or that elderly relatives are more likely to find themselves rejected. Certain recent developments such as high-rise flats have tended to contribute to the isolation of the family. The point needs to be made strongly that the family is not self contained and 'if this is forgotten the relationships and personalities within the family may be impoverished and spoiled and may well suffer from a kind of intractable and self-consuming density'.

Perhaps one of the greatest dangers to the family is that too much should be expected of it — that it is seen almost as the *only* instrument of good social behaviour and the *only* means of full personality development. There seems little doubt that the family gets blamed for too much: for crime, delinquency and antisocial behaviour generally. Alongside education the family tends to become a scapegoat for anything, for which we can find no obvious or suitable explanation.

But I feel that a note of optimism is appropriate to conclude this study of the family. It is impossible for the historian to judge the 'happiness' of our

61   The Royal Family still presents the ideal of family life to British soceity. It is a sign of the times that the royal group looks so much less formal than Queen Victoria and her family.

generation against those of the past, but the evidence we have suggests that in many respects families in all classes have advantages over those of the past. Certainly working-class families on the whole have never previously enjoyed the material comforts which they have today, despite the severe economic depression of the mid-1970s. As significantly there is a greater freedom in the family for children and women, and a greater emphasis on the development of personal relationships. Though a recent study in the USA has suggested that in America the working class put more emphasis on disciplining their children, while middle-class families stress the need for the individual development of the child, this greater freedom has affected all classes. Some would argue, of course, that this increased freedom is bad for the family and for the personalities within it, but while we may have lost something in the transition from the Victorian family to that of the present, one cannot help feeling that a good deal of the criticism of the modern family results from idealizing families of the past. Mr Macmillan's words, 'You've never had it so good', could well apply to the post-war family, though many a hard-pressed parent might find this hard to believe.

Further Reading

Michael Anderson, *Family Structure in Nineteenth-Century Lancashire* (Cambridge University Press, 1971)

H. S. Bennett, *The Pastons and their England* (Cambridge University Press, 1968)

Anthony Eden (Earl of Avon), *Another World: 1847-1917* (Allen Lane, 1976)

Ronald Fletcher, *The Family and Marriage in Britain* (Pelican, 1973)

J.F.C. Harrison, *The Early Victorians, 1832-51* (Weidenfeld and Nicolson, 1971)

Pamela Horn, *The Rise and Fall of the Victorian Servant* (Gill and Macmillan, 1975)

Peter Laslett, *The World We Have Lost* (University Paperbacks, Methuen, 1965)

Arthur Marwick, *The Deluge* (Bodley Head, 1965)

Alan MacFarlane, *The Family Life of Ralph Josselin* (Cambridge University Press, 1970)

H. Perkin, *The Origins of Modern English Society, 1780-1880* (Routledge and Kegan Paul, 1969)

Ivy Pinchbeck, *Women Workers and the Industrial Revolution, 1750-1850* (Frank Cass, 1969)

Janet Roebuck, *The Making of Modern English Society from 1850* (Routledge and Kegan Paul, 1973)

Lawrence Stone, *The Crisis of the Aristocracy, 1558-1641* (Oxford University Press 1967)

Roger Thompson, *Women in Stuart England and America* (Routledge and Kegan Paul, 1974)

Michael Young and Peter Willmott, *Family and Kinship in East London* (Penguin, 1962)

Index

The numbers in **bold** type are the figure numbers of the illustrations.